STRATEGIC INTELLIGENCE IN FUTURE PERSPECTIVES 2.0

Rodenberg Tillman & Associates Publishing International
Dwingelderdijk 47, 7991 RJ Dwingeloo, The Netherlands
www.rodenberg.nl / info@rodenberg.nl
Contact: Joseph H.A.M. Rodenberg at rodenberg@rodenberg.nl

ISBN 978-90-828227-0-0 (paperback)
ISBN 978-90-828227-1-7 (e-book)

Cover design: Löss Ontwerp, Amsterdam, The Netherlands
Editor: Dr. Michael Neugarten, Ramat Efal, Israel
Production coordinator: Drs. Ing. Alain Wille, United Kingdom

TABLE OF CONTENTS

"If a company is interested in finding the future, most of what it needs to learn is to learn from outside the sectors of industry", according to Gary Hamel.

However, how are you able to learn from the dynamics of change with all the disruptive technologies, if you are not able to watch it daily, 24/7?

Guess, how many companies do have a monitor or radar in place to make this happen?

One of the most-asked questions in business today is: Why didn't we see it coming?

ACKNOWLEDGEMENTS

I have been active in strategic competitive intelligence since 1985 as the founder and managing partner of Rodenberg Tillman & Associates. I would like to express my personal thanks to all the managers, professionals and business leaders across Europe, the USA and the Far East, with whom I have worked successfully during all those years. I have enjoyed every moment.

This book is the sixth in a series on how to apply strategic intelligence to the global business world.

In 2000, I published my first book, "Business and Competitive Intelligence, Management Discipline in the 21st Century", the first book to be published on intelligence in the Netherlands.

In 2004, my second book was published with the title "Enterprise Intelligence, Creating the Intelligent and Alert Organization". Its central message was the integration of business intelligence, competitive intelligence and organizational intelligence into enterprise intelligence.

In 2007, my third book "Competitive Intelligence for Senior Management" had as its key message, the positioning of the office of competitive intelligence on a par with other company functions that report directly to the board of management.

In 2012, my fourth book was published with the title "Strategic Intelligence in Future Perspectives". This was a compilation of seventy Intelligence Briefings, which we have been sending since 2005 to our connected network around.

In 2015, my fifth book entitled "Big Boys Big Ego's and Strategic Intelligence" was published, this time written with co-author Antoinette Rijsenbilt Ph.D. We looked at how narcissism can have both productive and destructive influences on organizational outcomes. Strategic Intelligence enables an organization's board of management to organize the necessary countervailing power.

This latest book "Strategic Intelligence in Future Perspectives 2.0" is another compilation of some ninety-five Intelligence Briefings which we have sent to our worldwide network since 2012. In this sixth book, my key message is how strategic management should be aligned with strategic intelligence: management cannot develop successful strategies without strategic intelligence.

I would like to express my heartfelt thanks to my wife Enyta and my children and grandchildren. Also, my special thanks to our leading business partner at Rodenberg Tillman & Associates in the UK, Alain Wille.

Joseph H.A.M. Rodenberg
Dwingeloo, The Netherlands, July 2018

I   PREFACE

"The essence of formulating real and different competitive strategies is relating a company to its external business environment", Michael Porter

It is always surprising to see that not that many companies are active in competitive and strategic intelligence. They still believe that it is sufficient to have departments of marketing, marketing research, marketing services, market insights, customer insights and more. Let us look at the schematic below, our "Intelligence Continuum". This is the key as to why the majority of companies get into trouble: they remain at levels one and two of the Intelligence Continuum.

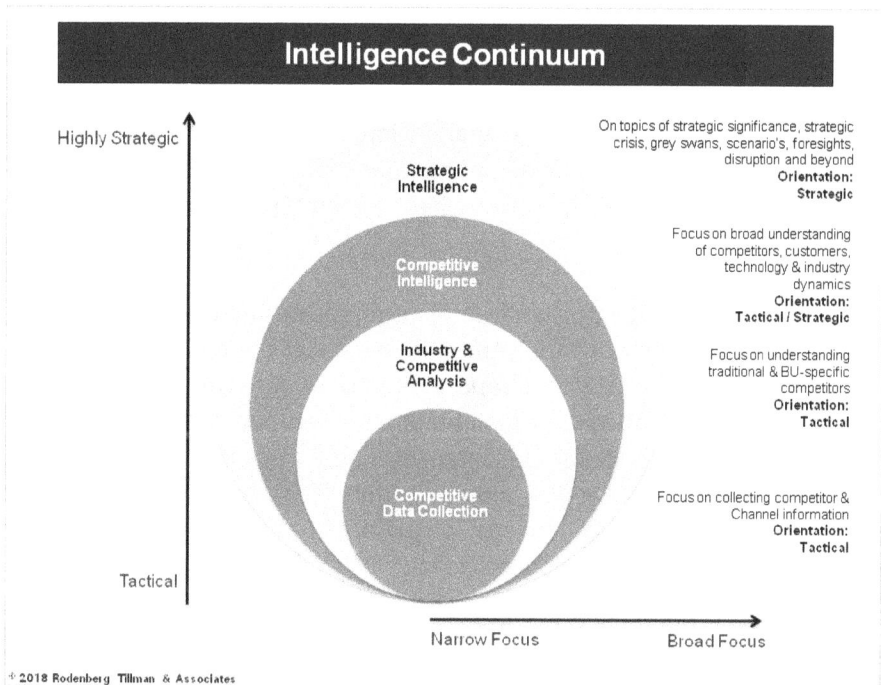

The four levels of the Intelligence Continuum represent the following:

1. Competitive Data Collection with a focus on the collecting of mainly tactical and short-term data and information.
2. Industry and Competitive Analysis with a focus on achieving an understanding of the market, of the competitors and other

elements in a particular industry sector. Again, this is mainly tactical and short-term.

3. Competitive Intelligence is the third level, with the aim of achieving a broad understanding of the current and future competitive landscape beyond the particular industry sector. This is a tactical move into the strategic area, but is still short to mid-term.

4. At the top we have Strategic Intelligence with a focus on the current and future competitive landscapes, connecting topics of strategic significance, strategic crisis, scenario planning, Grey Swans, Gray Rhinos and strategic war-mapping, with the aim of gaining timely insights and foresight to succeed in the future. This is purely strategic, and fully connected with strategy for the mid- as well as the long-term.

In most organizations levels one and two are the responsibility of departments and individuals dealing with market research, marketing services, marketing intelligence, market intelligence, marketing, customer insights, market insights and other functions that have become buzzwords. Those professionals deliver 'enriched information' which lacks real intelligence.

At level three we get into the area of competitive intelligence. It is a pity that in most organizations the competitive intelligence function is not on a par with other functions that report directly to the executive team and board of directors. Thus, any high-impact delivery of intelligence in most cases does not reach senior management. Raising this function to the level of other functions that report directly to the board is a vital precondition for this to succeed. If this happens, we are able to move towards level four and then talk about strategic intelligence.

With strategic intelligence at its core, company leaders get intelligence about potential strategic risks, business models that no longer seem to work or that have not adapted to changed market dynamics, potential opportunities for future success, surprises by Grey Swans and neglected Gray Rhinos.

In 2017 Dutch multinationals like Unilever and AkzoNobel became potential acquisition targets because they underperformed in the view of their shareholders. Kraft Heinz Foods showed an interest in acquiring Unilever, and PPG wanted to acquire AkzoNobel. They were not successful, but both

Unilever and AkzoNobel were forced to act: Unilever sold its Margarine and 'Spreads' business and AkzoNobel sold its Chemical division.

In his book "The Day after Tomorrow", author Peter Hinssen used four questions to clarify the problems faced at these and other multinationals:

1. Why are large companies blind to seeing new opportunities?
2. Why are large companies eager to buy start-ups, and why do they succeed in killing these start-ups in record time?
3. Why are large companies not able to make the right steps without outside support?
4. Why do large companies behave like 'lame ducks' when facing new disruptions, new business models, and new competitors and why they are unable to react more rapidly?

These four questions are not unique. We have seen similar publications in the last five to six decades. In essence, not much has changed within the business world, and most are still guided by inward-looking control-mechanisms. which is still a key problem in the majority of companies. What we miss are the outward-looking opportunity-mechanisms. We will explain the difference.

By inward-looking control-mechanisms are meant the management information systems, key performance management, control by KPIs, balanced score-card, business intelligence dashboards, risk management, internal audit committees, accountants, the board of directors or the old boys' network of mutual friends. Even all these mechanisms are incomplete. The aim is to control everyone, and in our strategic intelligence best practices we always ask: who is ultimately accountable? The honest answer is that no one is.

"An inside view is a breeding ground for all sorts of biases that consistently give more weight to the facts that back your view than the inconvenient ones that do not"

Outward-looking opportunity-mechanisms are the methodologies and techniques which enable us to align with the external business environment to get in control of the dynamics of change that our companies face.
Examples are strategy under uncertainty, strategy as active waiting, where-to-play/how-to-win, strategic war-mapping, Grey Swan analysis, Gray Rhino

analysis, technology play-mapping, Company Radar Room and others. Who is accountable here? It's the Tenth Man or Woman who leads the professional SEAL, SWAT, RRT (Rapid Response Team) or MI7 Intelligence Team. These teams challenge assumptions, lead with questions and tell management the brutal truth.

Ask yourself an honest question: how many of these outward-looking opportunity-mechanisms do we ourselves use in our company? We frequently hear that the SWOT-analysis is still used.

In November 2017 the European Intelligence Community SCIP gathered in Cascais, Portugal. SCIP is the Strategic Competitive Intelligence Professionals society and it was interesting to see which companies presented their best practices there. Amongst others, these included, Rolls Royce Power Systems, Metso Corporation, HPE, IBM Europe, Deutsche Telekom, Celfocus, Telefonica, Knauf Insulation, Travelport, Philips and Siemens. It was also interesting to see the presence of INSEP France, the National Institute of Sports, and the Center of Excellence of the Paris Olympics in 2024. It was remarkable to see that INSEP has a department of Competitive Intelligence, which is rather unusual for national sport organizations. Smart guys those French.

I have given some perspectives about strategic intelligence: acting at the top of the Intelligence Continuum which avoids many problems such as those listed with the four questions from Hinssen's book "The Day after Tomorrow". This implies that the focus of management should move from less 'inward-looking control-mechanisms' towards 'outward-looking opportunity-mechanisms'. One of the results will be the establishment of a SWAT, SEAL, RRT or MI7 team headed by the Tenth Man or Woman in the setting of a Company Radar Room.

In chapter II, I describe those perspectives in more detail … for the future.

Don't forget, the future started yesterday!

"It's easy to be wise after the event. That's the reason why we strongly recommend aligning strategic management with strategic intelligence"

II   INTRODUCTION

"It's naive to think you are able to develop strategy without strategic intelligence"

For some decades we have known that over 60% of innovation and disruption comes from outside our sectors of industry. Why then are we so stupid so as not to have some kind of monitor to identify the potential dynamics of change in good time? Would you fly in a plane without a radar? No, of course not. But in our companies, we do not generally use a company radar, do we?

It is the same with the vast majority of managers who think they do not need intelligence to do their work, whether it's sales, marketing, R&D, business development, market research, purchasing, compliance, risk management, customer services, or strategic management. Most rely on information from Google. Imagine that professional intelligence agencies were to rely only on Google. The world would look quite different.

A few years ago, PwC conducted some research among 1,800 business leaders in the US and Europe. They found that:

➢ Only 4% of all organizations are fully capable of deriving value from the information available to them
➢ 40% of all organizations do not have the necessary resources and skills to gain value from information
➢ 40% gain hardly any competitive advantage from their information
➢ 25% are unable to gain any benefit from their information

In the end, who is accountable for our being able to foresee change in a timely fashion? Different functions can do this; however, they may do so only partly and mainly in a reactive not proactive manner. Risk management is the responsibility of the risk managers. Big data is a different world populated by big-data analysts and data scientists. Strategic management in most companies is the responsibility of the strategists. Market research is the work of the market researchers, who in most companies are too far away from the level of senior management. That leaves marketing as done by the marketeers. Unfortunately, marketing has lost its position in the boardroom in the last 15-20 years. We might conclude that these kinds of managers are not able to take full accountability to foresee timely change. This is dramatic, and still leaves the question open as to "who is ultimately accountable?" Our answer: the Tenth Man or Woman.

II.1   The Tenth Man

The problem with most people is that they do not believe something can happen until it already has. This is not due to stupidity or weakness however, it is simply human nature. If nine of us look at the same information and arrive at the same conclusion, it is the duty of the Tenth Man or Woman to disagree. No matter how improbable it may seem, the Tenth Man has to start digging on the assumption that the other nine may be wrong. The Tenth Man delivers a mix of insights, foresight, and analysis, is able to develop strategies and is a strategic thinker. He or she uses other management tools than the traditional SWOTI (Strengths, Weaknesses, Opportunities, Threats and Issues) analysis. He or she uses unique strategy and strategic intelligence tools such as 'Strategy under Uncertainty', 'Strategy as Active Waiting', 'Where-to-Play and How-to-Win', 'Strategic War-Mapping', 'Scenario Planning', 'Grey Swan Analysis', 'Gray Rhino Analysis' and others. The results set possible courses of future action. Finally, this enables the Tenth Man to tell management the brutal truth they need to hear, and challenge their biases, assumptions and hypotheses.

Vice-President of Future Disasters

During keynote speeches on a wide variety of occasions I tell the audience that in one Global Top-50 company we succeeded in creating the function of Vice-President of Strategic Intelligence & Head of Future Disasters. In other international companies we were able to create a variety of teams such as SWAT, SEALS, Rapid Response or MI7, all under leadership of the Tenth Man or Woman. These teams must be positioned on a par with other functions that report directly to the Board of Management and Board of Directors.

Creating forward-looking courses of action

The Tenth Man or Woman and his/her strategic intelligence team creates the core basis where decisions are made based on evidence rather than on intuition. The challenge is to think differently from everyone else, because only this leads to future success. The Tenth Man and his/her team is not in the so-called 'me-too business'.

Their core activities are:

> - Analysis of the competitive landscapes beyond the traditional sectors of industry, outward-in and looking 1-3 years ahead
> - Setting the strategy framework: Where-to-Play and How-to-Win
> - Unleashing collective knowledge, the insights and foresight of key people. Executing Quarterly Strategy Reviews
> - Anticipating potential as well as existential risks
> - Establishing a new place to share, to communicate and set the courses of action: the CRR (Company Radar Room)

"There are decisions that can be made by analysis. These are the best kind of decisions. These are fact-based-decisions", Jeff Bezos, CEO of Amazon

Situation at Daimler, Lufthansa, Continental and Deutsche Telekom

Thomas Sattelberger's book "Ich halte nicht die Klappe" (I do not shut up) is a fascinating read. Thomas Sattelberger was a member of the board of management at Daimler, Lufthansa, Continental and Deutsche Telekom. Three remarkable quotes in his book are:
> - "Top management hear only their own stories"
> - "Employees are there to confirm these stories"
> - "We have taken the decisions and no one challenges them"

According to Sattelberger, German companies are autocratic, have a masculine culture, top management is not exposed to any countervailing power, the board of directors is a friendly 'old boys network', and mutual interdependence is huge. At the top there is no control, appointments come from mainly inside or from Deutschland AG, and the focus is still on "Smith looks for little Smiths". In Mergers & Acquisitions there is still the mentality of "Who has the longest little Willy".

Is the situation described by Sattelberger with these four leading multinationals in Germany different from that of multinationals in France, the UK, the Netherlands, Belgium, Spain, Italy, and in the other European countries? The answer is simple: no!

"The greater your responsibility as CEO, the greater the necessity to be humble", Pope Francis

Strategic Intelligence drives strategy

The majority of organizations still focus strongly on competing for the present and hardly at all on competing for the future. We have seen this in many multinationals which underperform. Examples include Procter & Gamble, Nestle, Unilever, AkzoNobel, Post NL, all of which were pressured by hedge funds. They hardly created any autonomous growth and waited like 'lame ducks' for things to happen. We saw a similar situation with Royal Philips in the years 2010-2015 with under-performance in the Electronics/Home Appliances, Lighting and Healthcare Divisions. Many hedge funds hedge funds made it clear in those days that the market value of the separate parts was much larger than that of the corporate company as a whole at that time. Philips divested its Electronics Division, and Philips Lighting got in addition to Royal Philips, with Healthcare as core, a separate IPO at the Amsterdam Exchanges.

The diagram below gives shows a clear view of the differences between competing for the present and competing for the future.

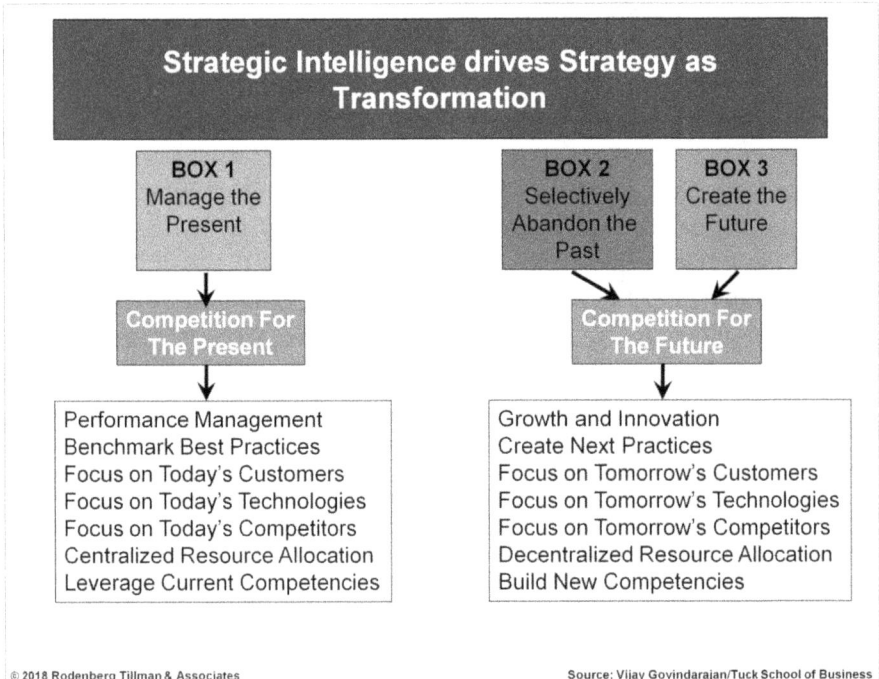

Strategic Intelligence drives Strategy as Transformation

BOX 1 Manage the Present		BOX 2 Selectively Abandon the Past	BOX 3 Create the Future

Competition For The Present	Competition For The Future
Performance Management	Growth and Innovation
Benchmark Best Practices	Create Next Practices
Focus on Today's Customers	Focus on Tomorrow's Customers
Focus on Today's Technologies	Focus on Tomorrow's Technologies
Focus on Today's Competitors	Focus on Tomorrow's Competitors
Centralized Resource Allocation	Decentralized Resource Allocation
Leverage Current Competencies	Build New Competencies

© 2018 Rodenberg Tillman & Associates   Source: Vijay Govindarajan/Tuck School of Business

If companies place too much emphasis on competing for the present it may take some time before senior management sees that their company is losing competitive advantage. Such companies then face a strategic crisis and the most commonly-applied actions are cost-cutting and layoffs. This is easier to implement rather than looking at potential new revenues. Note that it is always much easier to manage costs than to manage new revenues.

To manage new revenues means selectively abandoning the past and creating the future. Selectively abandoning the past requires active portfolio management which implies 'saying goodbye' to products and services which are moving towards the end of their life-cycle or do not fit well anymore in the company's future portfolio. Creating the future implies that management is actively engaging with tomorrow's customers, with tomorrow's technologies, with tomorrow's competitors, with growth and innovation and more. This is all about being outward-looking instead of inward-looking, or in other words managing of the status quo.

Dealing with outward-looking activities means having a consistent and continuous view of the dynamics of change in the external business environment. How can this be achieved? Not just by doing customer- or market-surveys or through activities by insight managers, or others with nice 'buzzword-named' functions.
The only way to do this is to move to the top of the intelligence continuum, namely, to strategic intelligence, which can give you the answers regarding significant future changes that will impact the existence of the company.

There are seven preconditions for success

The following combined aspects drive an excellent strategic intelligence capability:

1. Align leadership with strategic management and strategic intelligence
2. Take accountability to pull this all together and establish the strategic intelligence team
3. Develop and use non-traditional structured analysis tools
4. Identify the personalities and characteristics of senior management as the decision-makers of intelligence that cannot be ignored

5. Use non-traditional strategy models such as scenario planning, strategy under uncertainty, strategy as active waiting, strategic war-mapping and where-to-play/how-to-win
6. Get to the top of the Intelligence Continuum
7. Establish a CRR (Company Radar Room).

II.2 Strategic management

The figure below shows the most commonly-used diagram in strategy, and you may ask yourself why so many smart and well-intentioned people can get this so wrong time and time again.

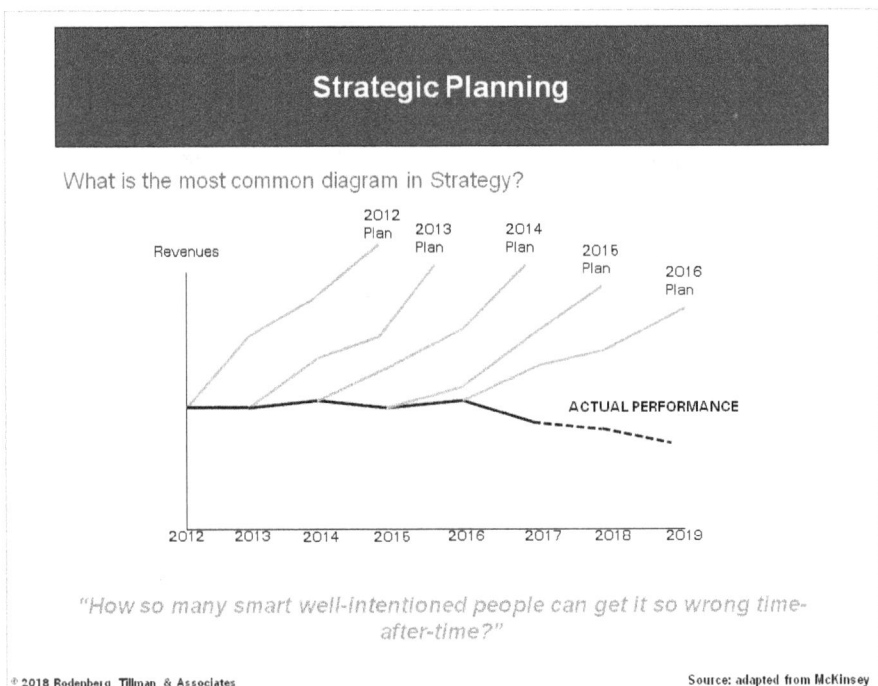

The first thing that worries me a lot is the misuse of the word 'strategic'. We hear and read daily in the media how the word 'strategic' is put into a wrong context. What they all mean is that it is seen as 'important'. No more and no less! The second thing that worries me is the lack of the capability to think strategically. Strategic thinking is one of the most difficult things in business. Which may be why so many smart people get it wrong so often.

Other reasons are overconfidence, and gathering data to support their own hypotheses (1), the fact that nobody gets promoted with forecasts that do not show an increase (2), creating over-ambitious visions to inspire great performance (3), resource competition leading to vying for their share of the capital spending budget (4), attribution bias – missed targets are blamed on the most convenient cause available, mostly a one-off event (5), strategic reviews that are lacking (6), a strategy process which becomes the set-up for next year's budget and KPIs (7), and finally hoping to get better results next year by trying to do roughly the same thing as last year but … just a little better (8).

"To be ahead of the game, multinationals have to learn as start-ups. You have to discuss everything"

What we see at most multinationals is that there are many managers who are busy with the traditional things. They all have in place inward-looking control-mechanisms such as key performance management with KPIs, balanced scorecards, business intelligence dashboards, risk management, internal audit committees, accountants and more. In addition, they have the monitoring guys, called boards of directors, or in other words their friends in the old boys' network. This is management of the status quo. The entrepreneurial drivers are gone and what is left are the shopkeepers, many managers acting 'under the radar' and even worse, many zombies. It is no wonder that many multinationals underperform: examples are Unilever, AkzoNobel, Nestle, Siemens, BP, Total, Danone, Vodafone, Dutch KPN, Post NL and many others.

In addition, we have another problem with the competitiveness of some ten percent of companies in the EU. These companies are unable to realize growth because the productivity rates are flat. According to OECD research dating from December 2017, extremely low interest rates in Europe in 2018 in Europe are keeping this group of companies alive. The OECD calls this group of companies 'zombies'. The implication is that good money, because of QE and low interest rates, goes to bad companies.

In our strategic intelligence and strategic management best practices we recommend five drivers to improve the companies' 'competitive readiness':

1. Understand your rivals' economics – think about the five biggest drivers
2. Look forward, not backward – future competitive reactions are widely ignored
3. Put yourself in the heads of your competition – execute strategic war-mapping
4. Synthesize into threats and opportunities – who has a sixth sense for Gray Rhinos?
5. Act more boldly – know your enemies and know yourself and in a hundred battles you will never be in danger (Sun Tzu)

"New strategic insights and foresight, things no one else does, are the differentiating drivers of competitive advantage. Strategic intelligence gives you the necessary evidence-based facts"

In the context of the same exercise we recommend management to answer the following ten questions to test the company's strategies (adapted from McKinsey/2017):

1. Will your strategy beat the markets?
2. Is your strategy based on the true sources of competitive advantage?
3. Is your strategy clear as to where-to-compete and how-to-win?
4. Does your strategy drive you ahead of trends?
5. Is your strategy based on privileged insights & foresight?
6. Does your strategy embrace uncertainty?
7. Does your strategy balance commitment and flexibility?
8. Is your strategy affected by biases?
9. Is there the conviction to act on your strategy?
10. Have you transformed your strategy into 'courses of action'?

These are great and simple questions, which are, nevertheless, a real challenge for many management teams.

Low-budget carriers

"Low-budget airlines determine the playing field of Air France-KLM", Pieter Elbers, CEO KLM, 12/2017

It is amazing to me that traditional airlines such as Air France-KLM, Lufthansa, British Airways, Alitalia and others have not been able to put up any countervailing power against the rise of low-budget carriers. The top-10 low-budget airlines like Ryanair, easyJet, Norwegian and others have been operating since the late 1990s. In 2017, the top-10 companies owned 2,300 airplanes, with another 2,250 aircraft in the pipeline at Boeing and Airbus. The simple message is to never, ever underestimate your competitors, even if they are very small.

"The sleeping giants like Air France-KLM, Lufthansa, British Airways and the other traditional airlines have been lame ducks. If you are running, competition will bite you. If you stand still, they will swallow you"

Banking and digitalization

Bankers still think that digitalization is about evolution and not revolution. Some 75% of bankers think that digitalization will not hurt their business models, and 80% of the bankers think that a smartphone app will be enough. Fintech does one thing excellently, while traditional banks do hundreds of things in an average way. Bankers feel themselves protected due to the heavy requirements of the monitoring agencies such as Fitch, and Moody's, as well as the FED and ECB, by the high cost of establishing a new bank and by the trust of their customers.

The tough competitive pressure for banks will come from the so-called 'hub firms' which will shape our collective future. These hub firms dominate individual markets. They create and control essential connections in the networks that pervade our economies. They form and control crucial competitive bottlenecks and they extract disproportionate value, tipping the global competitive balance. These 'hub firms' are Alphabet (Google), Amazon, Apple, Facebook, Microsoft and the Chinese giants Alibaba and Tencent.

In 2000, the market capitalization of the five largest US companies, then Microsoft-GE-Cisco-Intel-Exxon Mobil, was US$ 2,391 billion. In 2017, the market capitalization of the five largest companies in the US was US$ 3,373 billion: Apple-Microsoft-Amazon-Facebook-Alphabet.

So, we can see how the airline business has changed fundamentally, how banks face new competition by fintech companies and how the large tech companies dominate many markets. This has happened in a period of just 6 – 12 years and implies that we have to improve and prepare ourselves, and that we have to prepare ourselves and that we have to create the pre-conditions to foresee change in a timely fashion. "Seeing behind corners" shows us what the dynamics of change can be, with on top the Black Swans, Grey Swans, and Gray Rhinos, which enable us to see behind those corners.

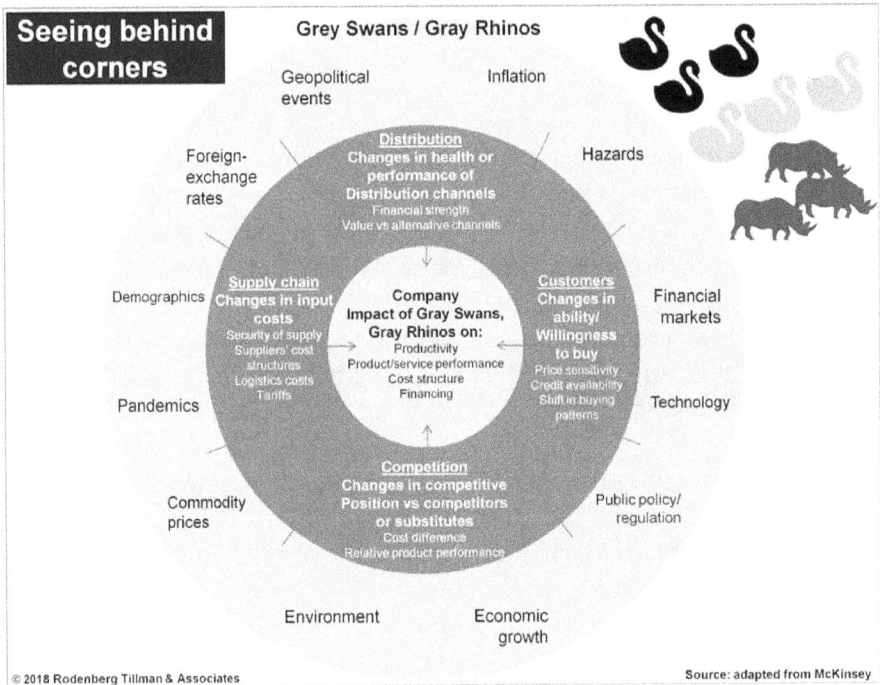

© 2018 Rodenberg Tillman & Associates   Source: adapted from McKinsey

"The more threatening externalities are facing a company, the more there is a need for Strategic Intelligence"

At the top right-hand side of the graphic "Seeing behind corners", you can see some Black Swans, Grey Swans, and Gray Rhinos. In 2007, Nassim Nicholas Taleb published his book "The Black Swan: The Impact of the Highly Improbable", one of the most impressive management books since WWII. In 2018, this book is still highly-applicable to everyone active in the business world. Black Swans are the "random events that underlie our lives, from bestsellers to disasters. Their impact is huge, they are nearly impossible to predict, yet after they happen we always try to rationalize them". Examples are a tsunami, huge storms like Sandy in 2012 and Irma in 2017, 9/11, Madrid 2004, MH17 and there is much more to come.

Black Swans – Grey Swans

In 2010, we added the phenomenon of 'Grey Swans' to the already famous 'Black Swans'. 'Grey Swans' are known, whereas 'Black Swans' are not. 'Grey Swans' should already be on the company radar. If not, management will always be surprised by external changes. We should have insights and foresight on upcoming 'Grey Swans'. There are many examples such as the game-changer of energy, the demographic time-bomb, instability in the Iran-Iraq-Syria-Lebanon region, Quantitative Easing by the FED and ECB, immigration, EU and the euro, 3D-printing, artificial intelligence and many more. Some of these 'Grey Swans' as well as other potential ones may have a huge impact on companies' existence. With strategic intelligence, management has the opportunity to be prepared for the potential scenarios of those 'Grey Swans', and always with the crucial question: what is the impact on our company?

Using 'Grey Swan Analysis', management can identify what the potential impact might be of those 'Grey Swans'. With such an analysis you can plot the high-medium-low levels of the impact of the relevant 'Grey Swans' against the level of uncertainty.

"The biggest threats facing management are not highly-improbable Black Swans, but highly-probable Gray Rhinos"

Gray Rhinos

The 'Gray Rhino' is another phenomenon in our strategic intelligence best practices. A 'Gray Rhino' is a highly-probable, high-impact threat, something we ought to see coming. You would think that something so enormous would get the attention it deserves. However, we consistently fail to recognize the obvious and so prevent highly-probable high-impact crises.

The problem is not one of weak signals, but of a weak response to these weak signals. We are bad at recognizing and responding to threats. It was the colossal failure of auditors, analysts at banks, investors and risk managers to recognize that a company valued at US$ 90 billion was merely a house of cards.

Heads of State, CEOs and especially politicians are so often weak at handling Gray Rhinos. The story of the Gray Rhinos is an excellent one, and so I was pleased to read Michele Wucker's book called "The Gray Rhino: How to Recognize and Act on the Obvious Dangers We Ignore".

Muddling around

In addition, there is a lot of muddling going on around Gray Rhinos. We muddle because of poorly-designed systems, lack of resources, weak leadership and a lack of accountability. We muddle for cognitive reasons like misperceptions, misinterpretations and poor motivation for acting on available information. We muddle, because it is easier to ignore the cost of not acting. We muddle to prevent much larger consequences: the harm of inaction versus the harm of action.

One example of the weak management of Gray Rhinos are the guys at the EU, since the crisis of 2008:
- Greece/banking   2009 – year-to-date
- Eurocrisis   2010 – 2012
- Ukraine   2014 – 2015
- Immigration   2015 – year-to-date
- Brexit 2016, Trump 2016, Catalunya 2017
- …… and there is much more to come in 2018 and beyond

We simply do not want to see. We avoid asking the questions for which we do not want to know the answers, because we do not want to deal with the consequences of knowing. This is especially so when inconvenient truths get in the way of stories we tell ourselves about how wonderful things will be if they go the way we have told ourselves they would.

Rhinos grazing on the distant horizon begin as distant threats. The closer they get, the higher the cost of heading them off. Gray rhinos have the potential to become herds and in the zoological world a rhinoceros herd is called a 'crash'. There are a number of biases related to Gray Rhinos. We list some of them here:

1. Optimism bias – overestimation of positive events and discounting negative events
2. Groupthink – the tendency to miss signals of any threats outside their normal expectations
3. Confirmation bias – we are less likely to consider and embrace alternative ideas which fly against conventional wisdom
4. Priming – the way we process information. We tend to overweigh information from 'experts'
5. Availability bias – our mental shortcuts that frame our decisions with the most immediate examples that come to mind
6. … wishful thinking, miscalculations, self-interest, perverse incentives, denial and more

Six stages regarding Gray Rhinos

There are six stages which help in dealing with future-obvious, highly-probable, high-impact Gray Rhinos.

1. Recognize the Gray Rhino – think, monitor the horizon, ask questions and avoid groupthink
2. Define the Rhinos – prioritize and frame them
3. Do not stand still – make big changes and muddle through if you must
4. A crisis is a terrible thing to waste – calamities can create unexpected opportunities
5. Stay downwind – act when the threat of the Gray Rhino is still far away
6. Become a rhino-spotter, become a rhino-keeper – one who recognizes an obvious danger that others ignore and who speaks up

"Rhino-keepers act against the crowd, knock down perverse incentives and inspire others. It takes courage to put yourself out there and sacrifice to avoid a disaster"

It is astonishing to see the complex strategies that people have developed to avoid recognizing information that could reduce the costs of a likely threat or create an opportunity. It is funny to recall when I am keynote speaker at various conferences and seminars, and mention as an example, the fact that we created a new function at a top-50 European multinational, namely:

Vice-President of Future Disasters

In 2016 Citigroup US created a SWAT Team to make disruption of Fintech happen

Strategic management and strategic intelligence

Competing in business means winning by beating your rivals. There is no end to the game, and there is no insurmountable lead. Competition has always time to catch up. Companies with the greatest market share often have a tendency to 'sit on a lead'. They take solace in their numbers, become complacent, arrogant and lose their competitive edge. Competing is an ongoing process of domination. The better you know your competition – their strengths, their weaknesses, their habits, their strategies, their tactics, their strategic intents and more – the better you will be able to dominate them. The crucial question is how much do we really know?

How are you able to compete in your competitive arenas if you do not watch your rivals, continuously, 24/7? Please, do not be naïve: your competitors are after your customers. Don't be naïve either, even if you think you have won the competitive battle. There is still the other much more important and crucial dimension of winning the competitive war. The difference between winning the competitive battle and winning the competitive war is strategic intelligence.

"Senior management should create its own 'intelligence staff' in preparing the organization for the future. In the military or at war, this role is called 'Chief of Staff' to the President or Prime Minister. CEOs and senior management desperately need such a chief of staff". In our intelligence practices we call the leader of the company intelligence team the 'Tenth Man or Woman'.

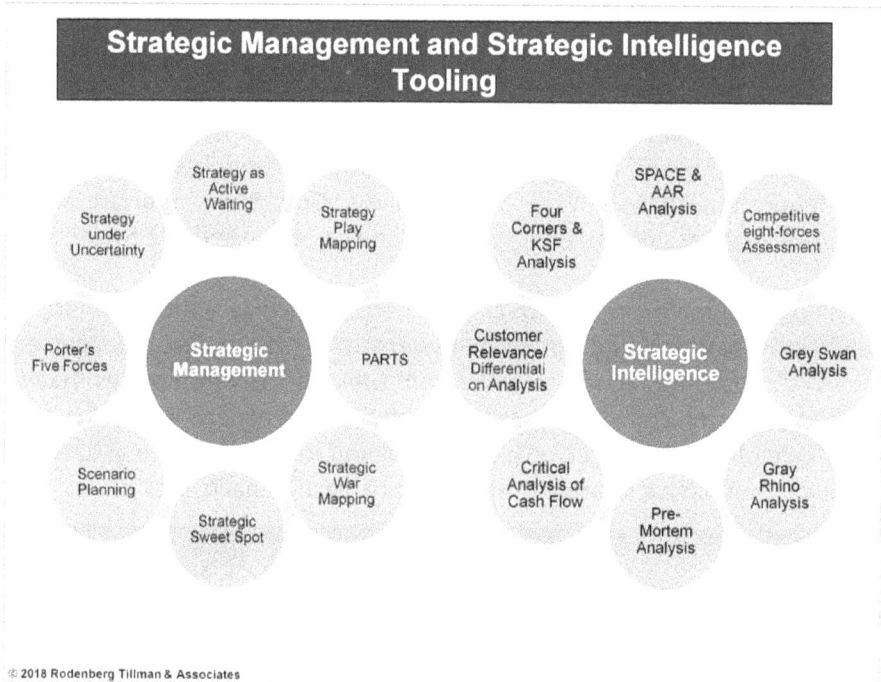

Strategic Management and Strategic Intelligence Tooling

Strategy as Active Waiting · Strategy under Uncertainty · Strategy Play Mapping · Four Corners & KSF Analysis · SPACE & AAR Analysis · Competitive eight-forces Assessment · Porter's Five Forces · **Strategic Management** · PARTS · Customer Relevance/Differentiation Analysis · **Strategic Intelligence** · Grey Swan Analysis · Scenario Planning · Strategic War Mapping · Critical Analysis of Cash Flow · Gray Rhino Analysis · Strategic Sweet Spot · Pre-Mortem Analysis

"Are companies like Unilever, AkzoNobel, Nestle, P&G, Post NL, KPN NL at the end of their company life-cycle?"

We can see that companies like those listed above are not able to outperform the markets anymore. Something seems to be terribly wrong. Competition is increasing with regional, smaller, decisive and entrepreneurial-driven companies offering alternative products and brands which are perceived as better by consumers. We already recognized some years ago that product managers, brand managers, marketing managers and all sorts of other managers aligned with 'insights' focusing too much on customer, consumer research, net promoter scores, and lost recently on big data and big-data analytics.

Peter Drucker, one of the most influential management consultants since WWII, always stated that companies have to execute two different strategies. The first is to defend their existing business with existing customers. And the second is to develop entrepreneurial strategies to meet unmet customer needs and meet non-customers. After all, the numbers of non-customers exceed by far the numbers of existing customers!

The "Strategic Management and Strategic Intelligence Tooling" chart makes very clear where the direction should be so as to become successful again. It shows the new road map of how to use new strategic management tools such as 'strategy under uncertainty', 'strategy as active waiting', 'where-to-play and how-to-win' and others. It shows strategic intelligence tools such as Pre-mortem analysis, Grey Swan analysis, Gray Rhino analysis, SPACE and AAR analyses and others. Make your choices and use these tools!

Challenge yourself, ask the tough questions, challenge your assumptions, lead with questions, and not with answers, to get there. Get management out of their comfort zone and away from their confirmation biases. Have a look at the graphic below and see the difference between "What they see" and "What they do not see". This is crucial and it is the difference between having or not having strategic intelligence in place or have not.

We like comfortzones and confirmation biases

Arguments   Facts

Logic

What We See:
financial accounts,
good performance,
successful stories,
positive projections to
the next quarters

Desires   Aspects

Habits

Fears

Attitudes

Values

What We Don't See:
outdated strategies,
loss of customers, lack
of innovation, loss of
competitive advantage,
unmet customer needs,
non-customers

"Don't just grasp the tip of the iceberg!"

26

Finally, the last step to make it happen with strategic intelligence and strategic management is to have it clearly visualized and communicated. To realize this, we have created the MI7 Company Radar Room, the CRR. The current MI7 Company Radar Room has nine large screens with the dynamics the company is facing, 24/7, and becomes according to our best practices, the New Board Room.

In the middle we have 'sales analytics', the daily bread and butter of the company. On the left are four screens with 'red alerts', 'pattern recognition', 'connecting the dots' and 'early warnings'. On the right are another four screens with 'AAR, After Action Reviews', 'trend mapping', 'new insights & foresight' and 'future action'.

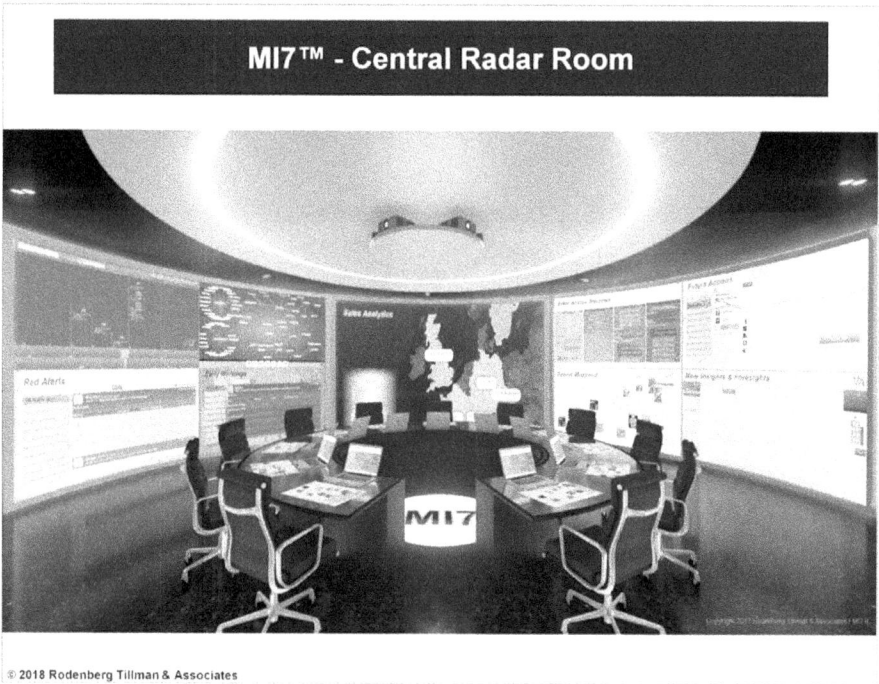

MI7™ - Central Radar Room

© 2018 Rodenberg Tillman & Associates

Wrap-up

A precondition for a successful strategic intelligence operation within companies is the combination of leadership-strategy-strategic intelligence. The challenges is to fight comfort zones, confirmation biases and zombies, taking accountability to put it all together, formatting the structured analysis tools, creating the Company Radar Room, identifying the personalities and characters at the top, co-creating the strategic where-to-play/how-to-win road map, positioning your team at the top of the intelligence continuum and acting as the Tenth Man or Woman by delivering strategic intelligence that cannot be ignored.

"The biggest hurdle for senior management is the acceptance of countervailing power by the strategic intelligence team, because this team delivers intelligence that cannot be ignored by tearing down the walls of senior management's biases, their unchallenged assumptions and their comfort zones"

III STRATEGIC INTELLIGENCE IN FUTURE PERSPECTIVES 2.0

Content

81. All too often we tell management what they like to hear
82. Exogenous factors drive growth in Europe
83. Critical questions and challenging assumptions are core in strategic intelligence
84. President Macron and the EU
85. Crucial questions in business today
86. Are multinationals at the end of their Company Life-Cycle?
87. Data defense and offense, and other crucial dimensions
88. Six reasons why managers have it often so wrong
89. Test your company's strategy
90. Jeff Immelt's lessons on leadership
91. Black Swans, Grey Swans and Gray Rhinos
92. The phenomenon of hub firms
93. Managing the present versus managing the future
94. The five drivers of competitive readiness
95. Inward-looking versus outward-looking mechanisms

1. Right-to-Play, Right-to-Compete or Right-to-Win Capabilities

"Assess opponents' conditions, observe what they do, and you can find out their plans and measures", Meng Shi

The above statement is straightforward and the marketers in your organizations should have the answers! Customers can make a purchase anytime, anywhere. Marketing is asked to do more to drive growth, with the same or fewer resources, while their spending is increasingly subjected to a new level of scrutiny. Most marketers try to tackle these challenges by spreading their bets across a variety of activities, a multipronged approach that leads to the incoherent use of funding, talent and other resources. Marketing organizations need to be strategic when it comes to managing their resources and teams. According to research conducted by Booz & Company, Korn Ferry and the Association of National Advertisers, two key priorities of action are relevant:

1. Marketing leaders need to narrow their focus, identifying ways to support the few differentiated capabilities that their company as a whole should pursue, to establish a right-to-win, meaning, the ability to engage in any competitive market with a better-than-even chance of success in the markets in which they compete
2. Marketing needs to hire and retain the talent that will support their role in developing these company capabilities

The big challenge is to invest more wisely in capabilities, whereby three separate classes have been identified. The first is to have the right-to-play capabilities, the basic functional capabilities such as campaign management, media buying and budgeting. The second is to have the right-to-compete capabilities, namely the capabilities to compete effectively within the sector of industry such as customer relationship management, format optimization (in retailing) and brand management. And the third is to have the right-to-win capabilities, which are cross-functional, complex, and reinforce one another, and are directly linked to the company's fundamental strategy of its 'way to play in the market' and so are relevant to all of its products and services. This coherent alignment between all the critical capabilities, the market and the portfolio, differentiate a company from its future competitors.

The Intelligence Continuum with the four different levels of intelligence contributes to these 'right-to-win capabilities' of organizations and concerns marketing intelligence (1), market intelligence (2), competitive intelligence (3), and strategic intelligence (4).

"Strategic intelligence starts with the executive at the top"

2. Early warning

"It requires courage to give countervailing power to inspired, applauded and obstinate strappers", Hans Zwarts

Imagine that your organization has a Company Radar Room which enables you to deliver the 'early warnings' that drive innovation, new market opportunities and business transformation, with the aim of getting to the future first?

Most of us like to hear what we expect to hear! Most of us are looking for and are able to understand the limited slivers of our positions within the market. The information that generates this understanding is myopic. We tend to discard the emergence of anything unanticipated or irregular. One of the big challenges in business is to scan the right data and information at the right time and foresee the changes at the periphery of our organizations in a timely fashion. Generally, we are very good at this. Ask yourself these three questions:

1. Why is the existence of a company not assured forever?
2. Why do so many companies face serious problems after many years of success?
3. Why doesn't management react even when the organization's success rate drops?

The answer lies in the failure to adapt, in good time, to discontinuous change. What happens is that strategic competitive advantage in the market is lost, which leads to pressure on sales/margins and thus cash flow, which then leads to problems of liquidity.

A Company Radar Room provides early warning before your brands, products, and customer solution services lose their unique positioning in the market place.

34

We are proud to have implemented such a Company Radar Room at one of the leading retailers in Europe.

"Genius is not in thinking up ideas, it's in executing them"

3. Politicians and the lack of courage

"Politicians keep throwing money to support weaker nations' debt problems, they never talk about restoring growth"

Both of the above statements come from Roger Bootle in Fortune Magazine, dated 8th October, 2012. Why should we listen to him, you may ask, as we read so much from so many economists, daily, about the problems across Europe? For two main reasons: Roger Bootle predicted the downturn of the 2002 dotcom bubble back in 1999, and the worldwide financial crash in 2007 back in 2003! He sees only one way to solve the European disaster: a breakup of the euro. And why? Because in his view Europe can only survive by regaining its competitiveness with a split in the euro.

Politicians and regulators such as the EU, IMF and ECB talk only about the huge overhang of sovereign debt, approaching and exceeding 100% of GPD in nations such as Greece and Italy. In this respect, the future competitiveness of countries is similar to that of companies. The PIIGS countries, namely Portugal, Ireland, Italy, Greece, and Spain, all suffer from a dramatic loss of competitiveness because of their excessive cost of production. In the PIIGS countries, the cost of labor has increased by an average 3-4%/year since 1999. This competitiveness gap was a decade in the making, the equivalent of 40%, compared to countries in Northern Europe! For example, Italy's share of global exports dropped from 5% to 2% since the end of the 1990s.

The PIIGS countries must revert to their former currencies immediately with devaluation rates ranging from -55% in Greece and Portugal, -40% in Italy, and Spain and -25% in Ireland. According to Roger Bootle, politicians have it totally wrong by continuing to throw lots of money from the public sector to buy time, however, the markets will win in the end. Abandoning the single currency is no longer an unthinkable choice, but the right one.

I am afraid, however, that our politicians in Europe do not have the courage to face this opportunity of future competitiveness. On the contrary, our politicians are very pleased to have been awarded the Nobel Peace Prize, which fills them with complacency!

"The euro is a depression-making machine"

4. The four barriers to interactions

"The truest characters of ignorance are vanity, pride and arrogance", Samuel Butler

Most localities have a few individuals who know many people across social and professional boundaries and facilitate networking amongst them. These people are called 'connectors'.

"It is amazing to see how the strategic intelligence solution of MI7 discovers and visualizes these new connectors in and beyond your sectors of industry and across the globe"

One of the most fundamental barriers that employees face across organizations today is how to improve the daily interaction between knowledge workers. Organizations around the world struggle to crack the code of improving the effectiveness of managers, marketers, sales people, strategists, scientists and others, whose jobs consist primarily of interactions – with other employees, customers, suppliers and stakeholders – and complex decision-making based on knowledge and judgment. Knowledge workers spend some 50% of their time on interactions!

Communities of Practice:

The power of MI7 allows organizations to create Communities of Practice to benefit from one another's advice, featuring online tools, using social-networking, sharing information-knowledge-intelligence, and sharing analysis tools during work in progress and beyond that too. Knowledge workers face four barriers to interactions:

1. Physical and technical barriers: these go hand-in-hand because of the lack of effective tools for locating the right people which can make collaboration difficult

2.	Social and cultural barriers: rigid hierarchy can prevent the right people from engaging for important knowledge sharing and collaborative problem-solving
3.	Contextual barriers: sharing and translating knowledge obtained from colleagues in different fields such as departments, divisions or business units
4.	Time barriers, or the perceived lack of them. Valuable interactions fall victim to time constraints. This must be avoided

What are the benefits of collaboration?

Imagine that the average salary of a knowledge worker is € 50,000 per year. This implies that € 25,000 is spent on interactions. We can estimate that the interaction productivity of this knowledge worker can be improved by 50%, meaning a minimum increase of € 12,500 in effectiveness. This is an impressive Return on Investment (ROI)! How long will organizations continue with static intranets, email overload, and time-consuming meetings, and continue spending a further 30% of their available time in collecting data and information?

Doing nothing might seem the easy way out. However, this is often an invisible mistake, a sin of omission rather than of commission. To act requires courage!

"Tough times don't last, tough people do", Nassim Nicolas Taleb

5. Strategic crises occur long before management sees them

"When the business model becomes misaligned from reality, it becomes a Trojan Horse. This is a destabilized business model and is caused between what it can do and what its environment demands", Trojan Horses of Decline

"Company decline occurs in three consecutive phases: strategic – earnings – liquidity. Early warning informs management that there might be a strategic crisis, which prevents the loss of competitive advantage!", Trojan Horses of Decline

The statements given above are crucial in today's business. Why? Because in over 95% of cases management lacks timely insights and foresight regarding potential strategic crises. The result is the rapidly-increasing pressure on earnings which results in cost-cutting and laying-off people. We read stories like this daily in the media, where top management explains that market conditions have changed, that customer behavior has changed, that new competitors with new business models have entered the market, or that a new technology was accepted much faster than initially thought. Who can we blame for this?

Management lacks timely insights and foresight regarding future change. There is a perfect solution to overcome this problem: Early Warning. Early warning can inform you about possible upcoming strategic crises for your company, which may lead to the potential loss of strategic advantage or strategic momentum.

The most misused word in business is 'strategic': Most people confuse 'strategic' with 'importance', leading to a misunderstanding of what 'strategy' really is. Strategy is not vision, mission, goals, priorities and plans. Strategy is the result of choices relating to where-to-play, how-to-win, and about long-term survival!

Early warning can inform you! Strategic intelligence-driven early-warning derived from your 'company radar' can provide you with the early indicators of disruptive changes about your target customers, how they buy, who they are, when they buy, what they buy, for whom they buy and from whom they buy. Here companies can lose their strategic advantages because they have been facing a strategic crisis.

Do you have a corporate radar, crow's nest or watch tower? We have created the most advanced company radar, crow's nest, watch tower or whatever you choose to name it. We call it MI7, which provides you with a platform to bring forward recommendations that are bold, not incremental, and that may be potentially unpopular.

Early warning challenges current information paradigms. Why is this?

- Because managers are generally more interested in information that supports their opinions than in contradictory information
- Managers are primarily interested in information regarding the business for which they are directly responsible

- Managers are primarily interested in information related to their incentive system
- Managers are more interested in information regarding quick wins or daily problems than in long-term business
- Managers have difficulties understanding what impacts directly on their businesses, and lack lateral thinking.

Do you recognize these paradigms? If so, you can imagine that early warnings may not often be welcome. However, early warnings derived from strategic intelligence solutions such as MI7 are needed desperately so as to ensure the long-term survival of the company!

"People do not lack strength. They lack will", Victor Hugo

6. **From integration to fragmentation**

"Integration in the EU will become fragmentation. Integration of divided regions in a country is the maximum in democracy. Don't do this with countries!", John N. Gray, Professor European Thinking at the London School of Economics, December 2012

Do you remember the 'three wise men' of the EU, Van Rompuy, Barroso and Schulz, celebrating their receipt of the Nobel Peace Prize in Oslo in December 2013? This looks like an example of toxic politics! Have they thought of new challenges to solve the European problem of high unemployment? Do they and European government leaders know what is really behind Europe's stagnation? The answer is a crisis of private investment which has decreased by some € 350 billion/year since 2007, equivalent to € 1,750 billion since the start of the financial/euro crisis. How does this compare to private and government consumption over the same period of 2007-2011? Private consumption is down by -0.2%, private investment is down by -14.5%, and government investment is down by -4.2%. But government consumption is up +5%, and net exports are up by +170.5%. Thank heaven for exports! The crucial challenge for the EU-27 is thus to stimulate/facilitate private investment!

"The politicians in the EU keep throwing money to support the weaker nations' debt problems and they never talk about restoring growth", Roger Bootle in Fortune Magazine, October 2012

7. Is Europe in crisis or is this more a question of chronic illness

"There is far too much negligence, failure and irresponsibility amongst the politicians in the EU"

The word crisis refers to a decisive moment or turning-point, which the euro never seems to reach. The single currency's complaint is more like a chronic illness that is neither serious enough to kill the patient nor weak enough to be easily cured.

Employment in the public sector: Is this a new time-bomb?

Employment in the public sector has exploded during the past few years, according to research carried out by IMD. On average, a country should employ not more than 15% of their total workforce in the public sector. What does the IMD research show us for Europe?

Countries with less than 15%: Slovakia, Luxembourg, Germany, Portugal and Italy

Countries with between 15% and 25%: Spain, Belgium, Romania, Republic of Ireland, Czech Republic, United Kingdom, Slovenia, Greece, Austria

Countries with over 25%: Finland, Poland, Bulgaria, Hungary, Estonia, France, Lithuania, Denmark, Sweden and Norway

In 2004 the public sector in France represented 22% of total employment. In 2010 this had increased to 29%.
In difficult times governments are tempted to create jobs in the public sector so as to soften levels of unemployment. However, in the longer term this becomes a deadly sin.

"The fall in private investment in the EU between 2007 and 2011 was larger than any previous decline. History tells us that it takes an average of 5 years to recover from such a drop in private investment", McKinsey Global Institute, December 2012

8. The role of strategic intelligence

"If intelligence is not driven externally, one is not doing intelligence"

Courage is necessary to make change possible. And intellectual courage is necessary to challenge conventional wisdom and the imagination of new possibilities. Leadership must refuse to accept limits or stop at industry boundaries. Lack of courage prevents positive change at all levels. Look at ineffective politicians who shift positions based on polling data, not on their convictions. Managers equivocate in response to new initiatives, observe struggles without support and without resources. When this works, they claim success, if it doesn't they say "I told you so". Individual decisions to hedge bets, hoard information or go passive reinforce the decline of businesses. This behavior is 'the timidity of mediocrity'. However, strategic intelligence is driven by practice, enthusiasm, motivation, inspiration and colleagueship to support courage. Challenging assumptions, and the confirmation bias, and executing the right analyses over and beyond our anchors, groupthink and risk mitigation, contribute strongly to being able to be ahead of the eye of the storm.

"Strategic intelligence must be 'on a par' with other functions that report to the board"

9. Black Swans and Grey Swans

"The more threatening externalities become for a company, the more there is a need to have strategic intelligence in place. Every company faces a continuous flow of threatening externalities"

This statement is clear to everybody. But to foresee those threatening externalities, companies need to be able to monitor them in a timely fashion. A couple of years ago, I gave presentations about the "Management of Insights" and the "Management of Foresight" at the Dutch National Marketing Insights Event. The audience consisted of around 200 professionals in marketing, research, strategy, and analysis. I asked the audience: which of your organizations have some kind of radar or monitoring system looking at the outside world? The answer: none! You should, however, have the Black Swans, the Grey Swans and your potential strategic crisis on your radar screen ready for action.

Black and Grey Swans!

Nassim Nicholas Taleb's book "The Black Swan" is an impressive read. In 2018, it is still highly-applicable to everyone active in business. Black swans are "the random events that underlie our lives, from bestsellers to disasters. Their impact is huge, they are nearly impossible to predict, yet after they happen we always try to rationalize them. A rallying cry to ignore the experts". How does this relate to strategic intelligence? Strategic intelligence is information that cannot be ignored! "If intelligence is not driven externally, then one is not doing intelligence."

What about the Grey Swans?

Grey Swans are known, while Black Swans are not. Grey Swans are already on our Company Radar Screens. Correct? We should have insights and foresight on upcoming Grey Swans: the eurozone crisis, instability in the Middle East, the fiscal cliff and the moment that China will sell its US-bonds. Do you have company scenarios prepared regarding these Grey Swans? In our MI7 Radar Room we plotted other Grey Swans, including the Global Currency War, the demographic time-bomb in Japan, the game-changer in oil and gas, Iran, the Federal Reserve and ECB on quantitative easing, the fall of China, the Straits of Hurmuz, 3D-Printing, and artificial intelligence. Have you plotted possible scenarios and do you know what to decide in the event that they occur?

Can you foresee your strategic crisis?

Companies facing a strategic crisis have lost their competitive edge. The problem is that in most cases senior management is unable to foresee this in time. Think of GM, Opel, Nokia, Motorola, Blackberry, TomTom, HP, Panasonic, Sharp, Sony, KPN, most European telecom operators, Dutch banks ING, ABNAmro, SNS Reaal, Philips and many more. The key reason why this is the case is that senior management does not accept objections because of success in the past, arrogance and complacency.
The key solution towards overcoming this phenomenon is to have the company's strategic intelligence capability on a par with other functions that report directly to the Board by creating a culture of "enabling truth to speak to power".

"The reasonable man adapts himself to the world. The unreasonable one persists in trying to adapt the world to himself. Therefore, all progress depends on the unreasonable man", George Bernard Shaw

10. Key Predictive Indicators

"As senior management accumulates knowledge, they rely more on their internal networks for information, growing less attuned to market conditions. The result is in favor of avoiding losses over pursuing gains", Harvard Business Review(HBR), April 2013

Do you recognize this statement? Think also about the Key Performance Indicators in your organizations, which are seen by management as essential tools telling them if their business is on target or veering off course. They are still, however, also tools for measurement. What should we think of these Key Predictive Indicators? This is about judgment, not quantity but quality, not costs but results. Measurement requires only a scale, while judgment requires intelligence. That is why key predictive indicators are a part of strategic intelligence and strategy, which raise questions rather than answer them. It is better to be approximately relevant than precisely irrelevant.

Key Predictive Indicators can include:

- Customer feedback: what do customers tell you
- Effective listening and communication skills; it's easier to teach reading and writing!
- Risk-taking, innovation and creativity: how often do people adopt new ways of doing things?
- Knowledge elicitation: meaning educating others so they will be able to generate their own knowledge
- Continuous learning: but people may leave? But what if you don't invest and they stay!
- Pride, passion, attitude, commitment: how can you measure these drivers?
- What percentage of your organization's time is devoted to improvement, and not simply performing the work?

- AARs (After Action Reviews), whose aim is not so much to correct things, as to correct one's thinking.

These challenging predictive indicators can influence our practice of strategic intelligence and strategy. We know that strategy is about shaping the future of our organizations. It is about setting in motion the sequence of events that will shape the future in a way our ambitions desire. There is, however, no guarantee that the future will turn out the way you want. It is explored with imagination, ambition and creative understanding of unmet customer needs and potential disruptive technology driving future opportunities. Take a deep dive why non-customers don't buy existing products or services? Think about new ways of providing value to non-customers. Challenge senior management with the question "why not change the rules, why are we still happy with the status quo, why do we still focus on short-term shareholder value, and why do we still lack long-term vision?"

"A clear strategic direction is a concise set of choices that determines what we do and don't do", Freek Vermeulen

11. Strategy is outthinking your competition

"Strategy explains how your organization, when faced with competition, will achieve superior performance. Competing to be unique thrives on innovation. Instead of competing to be the best, organizations can and should compete to be unique", Michael Porter

Strategy is about shaping the future. There is, however, no guarantee that the future will turn out the way you want. You can use strategy to figure out how to achieve your purpose and ambitions. You move between where you want to go (ends) and what you need to do to get there (means). A great strategy is the quickest route from means to ends to shape your future.

Strategy is also about outthinking your competition, about opening your mind to possibilities and seeing the bigger picture.
Strategy is about making choices differently from your competitors.

Do you know them? See the following ten key questions which will help you find out:

1. Who are your competitors?
2. What is your competition doing and what are their future goals?
3. Which of your competitors motivate you and why?
4. Who is doing the best work in your sector of industry and why?
5. Who is doing the best and most exciting work in any industry and why?
6. What would you do to improve your competitors' products and why?
7. What could the competition do to wipe you out and why?
8. How would you respond to the best/worst your competition could do and why?
9. What are the best companies in the world doing and why they are successful?
10. What are other companies doing better than you and why?

Are you able to answer these ten questions? Most of us don't readily invest in things that haven't yet proved themselves. Management is always busy with the day-to-day operations of the organization, and so a sense of urgency may be lacking to get the answers for these ten key questions. This is the case for many organizations that blindly follow the actions of their competitors. Examples are banks, insurance and healthcare companies, telecom companies, most FMCGs and others. How are companies able to compete successfully if they don't watch their competitors continuously, 24/7?

"Do you think you can do today's job with yesterday's methods and still be in business tomorrow"

12. Analysis is a precondition for creating Strategic Intelligence

"A new idea comes suddenly and in a rather intuitive way. But intuition is nothing but the outcome of earlier intellectual experience", Albert Einstein

Most decision-making in our organizations is still based on intuition and gut feeling. The aim of strategic competitive intelligence is critical thinking fueled by analysis and driven by perspectives over and above facts.

Analysis is key and is a precondition for creating strategic intelligence. In analyzing data, we tend to discern patterns early, jump to conclusions, ignore contradictory information or take other mental shortcuts. A good strategic intelligence professional knows intuitively, however, that there is always more than one credible potential future. Solid estimative analysis can provide these potential future trajectories.

In strategic intelligence we use four types of analytic spectrum:

1. Descriptive analysis: this includes arguments that are data-driven, reactive to events and give answers to the Who? What? When? Where? and How?
2. Explanatory analysis: this includes arguments that are slightly less reactive and identify the relationships between facts-events-observables-trends, giving answers to the Why?
3. Evaluative analysis: this includes arguments with the intent of assessing or establishing the meaning or implications of making judgments!
4. Estimative analysis: here the answers are given on what may happen next by giving the forecasts, foresight and future potential scenarios.

Two important characteristics of good estimative analysis are the capability to bound future trajectories and inform management of circumstances about which they don't need to be concerned. So, the key to success for strategic intelligence analysis is to imagine and portray the range of realistic scenarios.

One could conclude that strategic intelligence analysis is not that easy. It is like the difference between a pre-mortem analysis and a postmortem investigation!

"The truth isn't the truth until people believe you, and they can't believe you if they don't know what you are saying, and they can't know what you are saying if they don't listen to you, and they won't listen to you if you are not interesting, and you won't be interesting unless you say things imaginatively, originally, freshly", William Bernbach

13. How do we manage disruption?

"How can you make sense of the future, when you only have data about the past?", Clayton Christensen

How do we manage disruption? Or more importantly, how do we recognize its dynamics, anticipate its likely effects, develop and manage responses and sustain the necessary changes? Disruption can come in any number of forms. These include shifts in the dynamics of competitive advantage, technological breakthroughs, shifts in cost structure, new rivals entering markets from converging sectors, regulatory upheavals, economic downturns, idiosyncratic geopolitical and natural events, unforeseen internal company events, deregulation, re-regulation, and political turbulence.

For each company in every industry the first stage in managing disruption is to learn to anticipate and recognize the signs before this occurs. This is crucial to company survival. How can we recognize disruption before it occurs? Does the company have a radar to see disruption in a timely fashion? Does the company have an Early-Warning System in place? Does the company possess the capabilities that will be needed when the time comes to act? If the answer is no, then what does it have? Or will this be the oft repeated question in too many boardrooms be: why didn't we see this coming? One is far already too late if this question is asked, and there is no point trying to blame anyone but yourself!

Consider Nokia: when Stephen Elop became the new CEO of Nokia in 2010 he compared the company's situation to that of standing on a blazing oil platform. There was so much disruption that he stated that Nokia had to go faster, harder and more aggressively than the company had ever gone before. He left employees with two choices: "either jump into the water even if it's 100 meters deep and freezing cold, or get burned"; this was a clear statement that Nokia would be fearless in facing up to its dire competitive situation.

We all know many examples similar to Nokia facing such a dramatic strategic crisis. And new examples such as Nokia will surely occur in the future. What have we done to prepare companies to cope with such dramatic situations? We have a simple solution and it is simply called a company radar: MI7. However, we all tend towards complacency. One of the most famous examples of successfully managing disruption was published by Intel's founder Andy Grove. Entitled "Only the Paranoid Survive". This is one of the most impressive management books I have ever read.

"We have to go faster and harder and more aggressively now than we have ever gone before", Stephen Elop, Nokia's new CEO, in 2010

14. How to lead the organization through the dynamics of disruption?

"One cannot manage change. One can only be ahead of it. In a period of upheaval, such as the time we are living in, change is the norm. To be sure, it's painful and risky, and above all it requires a great deal of hard work. But unless it is seen as the task of the organization to lead change, the organization will not survive", Peter Drucker, Managing Challenges for the 21st Century

In the previous section we described how Nokia's market position in 2010 was compared with a blazing oil platform leaving employees the choice of either jumping into the water even it was 100 meters deep and freezing cold, or staying on the rig and getting burned. In 1996, Intel's Andy Grove of Intel published "Only the Paranoid Survive". Intel is the global market leader in semiconductors and rumors speculated that Nokia might be acquired by China's Huawei. Nokia and Intel both faced strong disruption. However, in the late 1990s Intel successfully managed to deal with this fierce disruption. Booz & Co. recommends three ways for management to successfully lead one's organization through disruption:

1. Preparation: anticipating potential disruption and putting those capabilities in place that will be needed if and when the time comes
2. Response: when a disruption occurs, management must develop the appropriate strategic and operational plans. These could involve be fewer products and services, launching new waves of innovation, business transformation or initiating M&A activity
3. Implementation: setting the response in motion and carrying it out sustainably to ensure that the company realizes its objectives.

Consider the following example of disruption: in the Netherlands the television sector is dominated by the Dutch Broadcasting Organization, the commercial channels/stations, the internet providers and the cable operators. Some years ago, two new players announced they were entering the competitive arena, which could cause disruption in the Netherlands: Netflix and Fox.TV. The key question was to what extent the current players were prepared? The success of a company's strategy often depends greatly on the strategies of its competitors. I had assumed that at least some of the current players would have had state-of-art Competitive Intelligence Capabilities as well as a radar for monitoring their business environment. However, they did not.

Our recommendation was: firstly, to find out what the current and future strategies were of your rivals in the competitive arena, and secondly, to fine-tune your own strategy and take a different position than your rivals did. One must start immediately and take care not to fall into the confirmation trap.

"The confirmation trap is what many decision-makers fall into when they look only for information that supports their hypothesis"

15. The competitiveness of nations

"Competitiveness analyzes how Nations and Enterprises manage the totality of their competencies to achieve prosperity or profit", Professor Stephane Garelli, IMD

This definition comes from my friend Stephane Garelli, who has, with his team in Lausanne, published the IMD "World Competitiveness Yearbook" every year since 1989. Nations and enterprises are in the business of managing a set of competencies and skills to achieve prosperity for the one and profit for the other. The Yearbook currently covers 63 countries and is based on 340 criteria grouped into four competitiveness factors: economic performance, government and business efficiency, and infrastructure. It was generated in collaboration with fifty-five partner institutes worldwide and is based on an annual Executive Opinion Survey of 4,200 respondents. Data are aggregated over a 5-year period. This is indeed great research!

At the Lisbon EU-Summit in 2000 our political leaders proclaimed: "In 2010 Europe should be the leading competitive knowledge economy in the world". However, looking at the facts and figures in the World Competitiveness Yearbook we can only come to the dramatic conclusion that our European politicians and political leaders have failed completely! In addition, at the EU we have non-elected, overpaid people like Barroso, Van Rompuy, Neelie Kroes, Olli Rehn, Catherine Ashton and another 22 members of the European Commission, a European Parliament without any power and a further 55,000 nice and overpaid public servants.

Do you remember those names by the way? We have never heard of them again. Below, we give Stephane Garelli's definition of the "competitiveness of a nation". All the EU countries have lost their competitiveness, except for Sweden and Germany.

The 28th country in the EU: Croatia

On 1st July, 2013, Croatia joined the EU as its 28th member. It has a population of 4.3 million of whom 1.2 million are retired. Of these 1.2 million retirees, 500,000 are veterans from the civil war. Some 2 million people are working class with an unemployment rate of 20%, a percentage which is expected to increase dramatically during the coming years. In fact, the economy of Croatia has collapsed, it is bankrupt and the country sees joining the EU as the last resort to survive! The profile of the country is institutionalized nationalism, corruption and no free press. Welcome to the EU-country number 28.

"The Competitiveness of a Nation is how a Nation manages the Totality of its Resources and Competencies to increase the Prosperity of its People"

16. **This won't happen to us!**

"If generals can't do without good intelligence, why do CEOs think they can?"

This statement is one of my favorites. Be aware that the vast majority of companies do not have a strategic intelligence capability in place. Almost every company may be surprised by changing market conditions and disruption.

Many sectors of industry see this coming, but don't, however, act in time. Examples of industries where this has occurred include the following: books, brokerage, telephone, newspapers, records, travel, and large box retail. Senior management tends to react: "this won't happen to us". We, however, know what happened, do you?

Future change and disruption will occur because of e-TV, e-Groceries, self-driving cars, pharmacogenetics, e-Health, domotica (home automation), bio-based innovation, 3D-printing among others. Have you already identified the upcoming Grey Swans in your sector of industry? If not, you may be surprised and your competitive advantage may vanish. If this happens your company will be in a 'strategic crisis' and the next step will be likely cost-cutting and layoffs of people. Why doesn't senior management see their own company strategic crisis coming?

Consider another example: Dutch National Telecom KPN has a subsidiary called XS4ALL, the leading internet provider for the Dutch business world. XS4ALL was the first internet provider in the Netherlands, founded in 1993 and acquired by KPN in 1998. At the end of June 2013, it was announced that XS4ALL would lay off one-third of their FTEs, due to pressure from cable operators UPC and Ziggo. Did XS4ALL-KPN not foresee the new pressure from these two competitors? Obviously not. Good competitive intelligence could, however, have informed senior management back in 2010 that this was going to happen and that XS4ALL would already face a strategic crisis in 2011.

TomTom. From 2008 onwards the consumer division known for its popular car-navigation devices lost an average of 10-15% sales revenues per year. Sales decreased year-after-year. TomTom was already in a strategic crisis in 2008 as their competitive advantage was under pressure. In June 2013, they announced the selling-off of their consumer division. But it is always easier for management to stay in their comfort zone. Right? Companies facing a strategic crisis can lose their competitive advantage 1-2 years before management gets the necessary insight!

Management fears new projects! In the Netherlands, some 60 percent of all new projects are rejected by management due to fear! Research shows that fear is seen as irrational. Only Ireland has a higher score of 82 percent, while Germany leads with a score of 24 percent. There is no doubt that such a high score in a country such as the Netherlands hurts innovation and change, and reflects a passivity about grabbing new opportunities. You probably recognize the arguments: how many customers are using this already? where has this been proven to be successful? can we see the track record? come back to us if this has proven itself with other customers. This all comes down to a fear of mediocrity!

"With Schindler's List I got the insight that one person, not an army, but one person can make the difference", Steven Spielberg

17. **There are more postdictors than predictors**

"Postdictors who explain things after the fact, because they are in the business of talking, always look smarter than predictors", Nassim Nicholas Taleb

As a result of hindsight, people who did not see an event coming, (think for example of Black or Grey Swans), will manage to convince themselves that they predicted it, before proceeding to convince others. According to Taleb, after every event there will be many more postdictors than true predictors. Think about this statement: "Never ask anyone for their opinion, forecast or recommendation. Just ask them what they have or don't have in their portfolio". Here are some related business case examples.

KPN Telecom: the Dutch national telecom company invested many billions of euros to expand into Europe to become a strong European player. But after 14 years, the company is back to square one in the Benelux, selling German E-Plus to Telefonica. It has itself now become an acquisition target for leading players such as Vodafone, Deutsche Telekom or America Movil. The Mexicans have already offered € 2.40/share. This is the best solution for KPN, where the board of directors failed completely during the last 14 years, with a drop in market value from € 70 billion to € 7.5 billion.

Vattenfall: the Swedish energy giant acquired the Dutch energy company Nuon for over € 10 billion in 2009. Just four years later Vattenfall had already written-off € 4.3 billion.

Air France-KLM: on 23rd July 2013, the Vice-Chairman of the Board stated in the National Dutch Financial Newspaper: "The problem in air traffic for short distances is Europe. Something must be done". Air France-KLM is losing money and more restructuring rounds of cost-cutting will follow. This reminds me of the airline business sector in the 1990s which was arrogant and complacent, neglecting the pioneer Laker Airways, and later the entrepreneurs behind Virgin Airways, Ryanair, easyJet, Southwest Airlines, Norwegian and others.

Stelios Haji-Ioannou: do you remember the entrepreneur and founder of easyJet, who started out with an easyFoodstore in the UK, challenging Aldi, Lidl and Asda? The name of the new store was to be easyFed, a "supermarket for the poor". Did you know that he also founded FastJet, a new airline for popular destinations in Africa? Jeff Bezos, the CEO and founder of Amazon, has personally acquired The Washington Post. It will be interesting to see what this great entrepreneur with his 'web genes' is planning to do with this 'paper'!

Can you see the differences between KPN, Vattenfall, Air France-KLM and the founders of Virgin, Ryanair, easyJet, Southwest Airlines and guys such as Stelios Haji-Ioannou and Jeff Bezos? Nassim Nicholas Taleb calls this crucial difference "soul in the game". Taleb has also put this phenomenon in another context:

"There is no other way to produce a forecast without being a turkey somewhere, particularly in the complex environment in which we live today", Nassim Nicholas Taleb

18. False decisions at Philips, Shell, ING Bank and DNB

"We cannot solve our problems with the same thinking we used when we created them", Albert Einstein
"Information that cannot be ignored does not come from databases, IT-systems or from the internet. It is the result of analysis"

As you can see from the statements above, one cannot do today's job with yesterday's methods and expect to be in business tomorrow! Do you want to learn new methods, new insights and foresight, new perspectives, and techniques, to get motivated, inspired and learn how to compete successfully in the future? Why is this of importance? The best ideas in the world are not in your head, your organization, or your industry: most come from looking around.

Here are some interesting perspectives we would like to share with you:

- The CEO of Philips stated: "It's not because the circumstances are currently not good, but because of the lack of belief and the willingness to take risks and to walk an extra mile. If we stay in the harbor we get nowhere. So let's take our sailing boat and look for the wind. Too many people behave as managers and we have to push them more into the direction of entrepreneurship"
- The CEO of Shell admitted that it was wrong to invest $ 24 billion in shale gas and oil in the USA. It seems that Shell entered this market far too late. The Shell's CEO has since left the company
- The CEO of ING admitted that it was a fundamentally wrong decision to integrate banking and insurance in 1991. Banking and insurance have different dynamics, the speed is different and the people are different. The CEO has since left the company
- The CEO of DNB, The Dutch National Bank, stated that the Netherlands will emerge from the economic crisis because of his good feeling on some indicators. He classified this as "anecdotal evidence"
- More than 60% of the Top-25 listed Dutch multinationals have lost on competitiveness based on ROI, on profit potential, on the consistency of results and on future growth expectations, according to international research from Accenture. This includes companies like Unilever, DSM, Philips, ArcelorMittal and Shell

"Most managers are not able to make the connections. They collect information from Google and don't understand the context. That's not knowledge, that's information", Rob de Wijk, University of Leiden

19. **Most systems are down and we still accept it**

"Now it is time for new ideas because all systems are down: government, hospitals, housing corporations, energy-, insurance-, telecom companies and banks have a serious lack of new ideas and energy. It's all about money and earning money and no longer about why those institutions were ever even founded", Terts Brinkhoff

How can these systems-based organizations survive, when inspiration, passion, enthusiasm, motivation have faded away a long time ago? These organizations now jump on 'big data', however, although big data can gradually improve our abilities as we work with it, it does not grant instant omniscience, and is not an automatic cornucopia or substitute for insight. We have a much more crucial phenomenon available to us these days, 'open data'. The volume of open data, machine-readable information, encompasses huge volumes of unstructured information which cannot be handled by mankind. According to McKinsey, open data is in its early days, but has, however, significant economic value. Unlocking this volume of information could create an estimated annual economic value of between US$ 3 - 5 trillion, not billion!

'Open data' breaks down information gaps across industries which enables organizations to propel innovation, improve new products, uncover anomalies, and replace traditional and intuitive decision-making with decision-making driven by intelligence. It is the essence of creating future perspectives beyond simply the facts.

The world's leading consultancy firm states that this phenomenon is in its early stage. Some of our clients, however, already work with such an 'open-data killer', MI7, with killer-apps in the management of unstructured information such, as early pattern-recognition, connecting liquid information and semantic analysis.

"An amazing number of people offer an amazing amount of value over networks. But the lion's share of wealth now flows to those who aggregate and route those offerings, rather than those who provide raw materials", Jaron Lanier

20. Banks: misplaced, misleading, and mistaken false arrogance

"Banks consistently use false arguments to overcome strong regulations: Misplaced, Misleading and Mistaken", Anat Admati, Professor of Economics at Stanford's Graduate School of Finance

In November 2013, Professor Admati was in Amsterdam presenting her book "The Bankers' New Clothes" and speaking about the false lobby of the Dutch National Employer's Organization VNO-NCW on Dutch banks. The professor sees herself as "a voice in the wilderness" because banks in the Netherlands and Europe want to keep to the 3% requirement of equity on total assets. She listed twelve reasons why politics must force banks to change now:

1. The current 3% requirement of equity on total assets must increase to 20-30%
2. It is a fundamental mistake that because of these higher capital requirements banks should no longer be able to give loans, credits and mortgages. On the contrary, it is the shortage of capital that limits the granting of credits
3. Banks argue that economic growth will suffer. They should ask themselves why Europe in 2013 is still in crisis following 2008
4. Banks made the wrong decision to prefer to give loans to Greece instead to companies
5. Governments disturbed the granting of credits because they also wanted banks to give loans to Greece and other countries instead of to companies
6. Many banks in the EU have a portfolio of huge bad loans/debts. Do politicians have the courage to solve these huge problems at so many weak performing banks in the EU?
7. Banks must be forced not to continue to pay out dividends, but should instead use profits to strengthen equity
8. If banks become smaller, it will become easier to get new capital. Banks are too big, not at all efficient, difficult to manage and difficult to regulate

9. There is no alternative to strengthening capital positions, because banks are still only viable with government support. Take the example of the rescue of two Italian banks by the Italian Central Bank in 2017
10. Support or subsidies by governments stimulates perverse behavior, perverse growth and inefficient size
11. The European Commission wants 'bail-in', however the thrust of the Commission should be prevention, preventing situations where the tax-payers have again to save the banks
12. Banks still think that equity should be seen as 'dead money', preventing them from giving loans, credits and mortgages. In this way banks like to continue to frighten both politicians and society

Consider the following example: It is amazing that the Dutch National Bank, DNB, does not want to recommend equity above 4%. This is unrealistic, and since 2008 we have seen that the DNB lacks the real courage to act towards banks such as ING, ABNAmro or Rabo Bank. This means that those banks, 'too big to fail', still misuse their position in the marketplace. If banks are not forced to increase equity to at least 10%, taxpayers will have to save them again when the next financial crisis occurs.

"It's insane that banks still pay dividend to shareholders. By doing this, capital is flowing off; it should, however, be used to strengthen their own equity", Professor Anat Admati

21. It's an illusion that you are able to keep pace with all changes

"Companies must become much more alert, otherwise they will lose out. Firstly, you have to disrupt your own business model. Secondly, if you are dependent on innovation within your own company, you are dead", Peter Diamandis

Peter Diamandis founded the prestigious US Singularity University, active in research on new technologies and author of the bestseller "Abundance". One of his visions is that technology developments do not just follow the linear curve of growth, but do, however, follow the curve exponentially. Many Boards underestimate the speed of technology change and when this happens exponentially the company loses ground. There are numerous examples where this occurs, the latest being Blackberry and Nokia.

This is why so many companies are surprised by the dynamic changes taking place in their business environment.

Linear versus exponential growth is an illusion.

The problem is that people think linearly, so management has to watch what is really happening and what will happen in their business environment much more carefully. It is an illusion that a company's employees are able to keep pace with all changes. Even successful companies like Google, Amazon, Apple, Samsung, IBM and others cannot keep pace and have created the insight that there are always more smart people outside than inside their companies.

40% of the Top-500 Fortune companies will be gone in 2021:
Companies have to monitor what is going on at the periphery of their industrial sectors, since this is where you can expect disruption. Flexibility and maneuverability are the preconditions to survival. The average life span of Top-500 Fortune companies has decreased from 67 years in 1920 to 15 years in 2012, according to Yale University. The US-based Olin Business School conducted research in 2011 that showed that at the current rate of technology change, 40% of the Top-500 Fortune companies will have disappeared by 2021.

Is this relevant in the Netherlands? Please wake up!
We often hear the argument that many companies that haven't been able to keep pace are 'merely' foreign companies. But please just wake up! Since 2000, the following Dutch multinationals have disappeared: Fortis Bank, Corporate Express, Royal Hoogovens, Getronics, Hagemeyer, Numico, Nedlloyd, Vedior, VNU, Stork, Draka, Crucell, Royal Wavin, Martinair, Essent, Nuon, and Douwe Egberts. Both SNS Bank and ABNAmro became state-owned, ING and Rabo Bank faced huge problems, and KLM Airlines generates profits for Air France, and has been doing so for many years.

"It's an illusion that employees of a company are able to keep pace with all changes", Peter Diamandis

22. **Banks, business as usual**

"We see that banks try to improve their ratio's by shifting risks. However, these risks stay within the financial system. The system risks have not been reduced, and have in fact increased", The Centre for European Policy Studies

Can you imagine that five years after the financial crisis, the financial system in Europe has still not yet improved? Banks still continue to package 'risky financial products' into special entities. Our bankers still behave the same as they did before the financial crisis. Why is this so? Bankers think they are better protected against the next financial crisis, because they have a higher percentage of equity on total assets. It's business as usual all over again.

Equity on total assets
In November 2013, we could read that some fifteen banks were fined billions of euros because of Libor-gate and the forming of cartels. Research from the European Banking Authority showed that there were around 4,000 bankers in Europe who earned more than € 1 million in 2012. These numbers are growing! Another remarkable issue is that banks in Northern Europe in countries such as Belgium, Finland, Germany and The Netherlands, are much weaker than banks in Southern Europe. Why is this? Because the top management of the banking system in Northern Europe knows that their governments will rescue them when the next financial crisis occurs: they are too big to fail. The International Standard of 'equity on total assets' is just 3%: the EU wants to increase this to 4%. In Section 20, we listed twelve arguments from Professor Anat Admati at the Stanford Graduate School of Finance as to why this should be increased to 20-30%.

The role of politicians?
Politicians have not generally shown much courage. This is because they assume that during the next crisis the large bond holders and savers will have to pay via 'bail-in'. But this is a false assumption, which will not happen. And this is because during the next financial crisis a 'bail-in' will cause a huge domino effect. Politicians try to control banks with more and more regulations, and banks continue to circumvent these regulations. Business as usual.

There is, however, a solution.

The solution to overcoming the next financial crisis

The ultimate solution is not to split banks into retail and investment banking, but rather into domestic and international banking. This will force the bankers to go back to serving their customers at both a regional and local market level. It is time to change, and time for new ideas, because all systems are down whether at governments, hospitals, housing corporations, energy/insurance/telecom companies or at banks. Each of these sectors is suffering from a serious lack of new ideas, energy and passion. They are all focused on money and earning more money and no longer on the ideas for which these institutions and organizations were originally founded.

New Grey Swan

In 2007, Nassim Nicolas Taleb published his hugely successful book "The Black Swan". Black swans are large-scale unpredictable and irregular events which have massive consequences. It is not feasible to prepare ourselves for Black Swans. But we can, however, prepare ourselves for Grey Swans. These are events which have a very high impact, but for which organizations are able to prepare themselves.

The current banking system with far too low percentages of 'equity on total assets' is not simply a Grey Swan, it is a huge Grey Swan.

"Postdictors, who explain things after the fact, because they are in the business of talking, always look smarter than predictors", Nassim Nicolas Taleb

23. Outthinking competition

"Being overtaken by competitors is your worst nightmare" – "It is never too late to listen", Beeckestijn Business School, The Netherlands

You will have the ability to outthink your rivals in the marketplace if your company is able to observe emerging trends before its competition does. A key challenge is to organize the early warning signs of critical changes. You have to ask yourself: (1) what market developments should we be looking for? (2) what are the leading indicators before these developments appear? (3) are we able to observe these leading indicators? and (4) where can we track this information and how can we monitor it?

How not to do this?
In the majority of organizations, common daily practice is to use information on the web to find documents and other sources of data and information relevant to the topic, select the best sources within one's comfort zone, gather the most relevant information, copy and paste the bits and pieces of the information, and then edit the compilation thereby creating a report. Rob de Wijk, Professor of Strategic Studies at the University of Leiden has a highly-applicable comment which relates to this: "Most managers are not able to make the connections, they collect information from Google and don't understand the context: That's not knowledge, that's just basic information". Do you want to challenge yourself and management?

"Here the success of everything depends on … seeing things in a way which afterwards proves to be true, even though it cannot be established at the moment…", Joseph Schumpeter

24. The leverage ratio of banks is far too low

"If I had asked people what they wanted, they would have said faster horses", Henry Ford

"The best way to predict the future is to invent it", Steve Jobs (2011)

We have reported on the continuous threats to banks, and have identified that these are not Black, but Grey Swans. Black swans are large-scale unpredictable and irregular events of massive consequence for which we hardly can prepare ourselves. Grey Swans, on the other hand, are events which have a very high impact, but one for which organizations are able to prepare themselves. Banking is such a huge Grey Swan. Why is this?

The Leverage Ratio?
The Leverage Ratio for Banks, or their Equity on Total Assets must be at least 3%.

The EU/ECB wants to increase the Leverage Ratio to 4%. And Swiss and US banks already are close to a Leverage Ratio of 9-10%. However, many banks in Europe still have a value of only 2%. Imagine that you are an entrepreneur and you want to raise capital or get a loan from a bank: those same banks will, as a precondition, ask you for a Leverage Ratio of at least 40-50%.

Where is the new Grey Swan? By January 2014 the authorities gave banks a green light that the Leverage Ratio no longer applies to Total Assets, but on total assets whereby the left side and the right side of the balance sheet of similar assets are cleaned-up. So, the Leverage Ratio is related to lower total assets to get higher percentages of the Leverage Ratios. This implies that the Leverage Ratio is related not to gross total assets, but to net total assets. This reduces the financial liabilities of banks by around 60%! According to our research this is a huge Grey Swan having a very high potential negative impact.

New funding to save banks?
Closely related to this is new special funding of some € 55 billion created by the ECB; by 2026, banks in deep trouble could perhaps rely on this. Take into account that the total assets of all banks in the EU is € 30,000 billion, and bear in mind, for example, the largest bank in France, Credit Agricole, has total assets of € 2,000 billion. We might conclude that during a second potential financial crisis (the first was from 2008-2013), banks, politicians and the EU/ECB will once again rely heavily on European taxpayers who will, again, be called upon to solve the next financial crisis. Business as usual!

What is the new challenge?
This Grey Swan will be of considerable impact and there will certainly be more Grey Swans. The challenge for management today is to identify all those Grey Swans which may have a future impact on the organization. It is better be prepared than to be surprised. This reminds us of Peter Drucker who stated over 50 years ago: "There are companies that make things happen, there are companies that watch things happen and there are companies that wonder what happened?"

"We need in Brussels more courage, more leadership. However, by showing more courage and leadership they are not re-elected", Paul Polman, CEO of Unilever

25. **Too many companies like the comfort zone when working on strategy**

"All executives know that strategy is important. But almost all find it scary, because it forces them to confront the future they only can guess at"

"Strategic plans become the budget descriptive front-end, projecting 5 years ahead. But management only commits to year one. In the context of 2-5 years, strategic means impressionistic"

Choosing a strategy entails making decisions that explicitly cut off possibilities and options. It is a natural reaction to make the challenge less daunting by turning it into a problem that can be solved with tried and tested tools. The strategic plan is supported with detailed spreadsheets that project costs and revenues quite far into the future. At the end of this strategy process everyone feels much less scared; so this is about coping with fear of the unknown. But it is not the right way to make strategy. True strategy is about placing bets and making hard choices, not so much to eliminate risks but to increase the odds of success and of getting out of one's comfort zone.

There are three comfort-zone traps:

1.   Strategic planning: all strategic plans tend to look pretty much the same; first come the vision, mission and goals; then a list of initiatives; and then conversion into financials. The plan consists of whatever initiatives fit the company resources. It does not challenge assumptions or unmet customer needs
2.   Cost-based thinking: costs fit perfectly to planning because they are under the control of the company. Costs are also comfortable to work with because they can be planned with relative precision. For costs, the company makes the decisions, while for revenues it is the customers who make them. Revenues are not under the company's control, and therefore unknowable, nor are they

controllable. Planning, budgeting and forecasting are therefore impressionistic exercises

3. Self-referential strategy frameworks: here we have to be aware of the deliberate, intentional, and emergent strategy which consists of the company's responses to a variety of unanticipated events. Managers overestimate their ability to predict the future. It is crucial to watch carefully for the dynamics of change in the competitive environment.

To escape from one's comfort-zone traps, the following considerations should be taken into account:

1. Give the answers on both choices which determine success: Where-to-Play and How-to-Win
2. Strategy is not about perfection: strategy is primarily about revenues rather than costs and perfection is an impossible standard. Strategy shortens the odds of a company's bets
3. Make the logic explicit: what do you need to believe about customers, about the evolution of your sector of industry, about competition, about the future competitive landscape and about your own capabilities?

If a company is completely comfortable with its choices, it is at risk of missing important changes in the competitive landscape. The consequence is that companies may run into a strategic crisis. Examples of such companies are numerous: Opel, PSA Peugeot Citroën, Nokia, Blackberry, Panasonic, Sharp, Sony, Philips, KPN, ING, ABNAmro, Rabo, SNS, PostNL, TomTom, Capgemini, Atos, Imtech and many more. All these companies lost their competitive edge by competing for the present rather than competing for the future. (Part of this section was based on a publication on strategy in HBR J/F 2014).

"Thirty percent of participants in any strategy discussion should be under the age of 30, because they are not wedded to the past", Narayana Murthy of Infosys India

26. **Companies compete in arenas, not in sectors of industry**

"Management must step back from the day-to-day hustle and ask the right questions. Are there new competitors from unexpected places? What barriers to entry are coming down? Where are there cheaper substitutes?"

"Competing in arenas needs new information systems that give the insights and foresight on what is going on in those arenas. Your current management information systems don't give you this!"

Both the above statements are by Professor Rita McGrath of US Columbia Business School, whose book "The end of competitive advantage" was published in 2013. Management needs to get out of its defensive mode and must be open to intelligence and welcoming to news, even if it is bad news. Companies need different systems for managing their core business and for managing new opportunities. Industry analysis is part of the core business, while arena analysis deals with new opportunities. If you compete in arenas, you need information systems that give you a line of sight into what is going on in those arenas, and management needs to be able to move resources quickly, according to McGrath. She lists the following ten new dimensions as necessary to create temporary competitive advantage:

1.   Leveraging assets is the new phenomenon
2.   Reorganization versus consistently changing structures
3.   Information efficiency versus information effectiveness
4.   Flexibility over optimization
5.   People who are educable, rather than people who are deeply specialized
6.   Competitive position is about arenas rather than sectors of industry
7.   Competition comes from other industries
8.   Reframe where the company adds value and where it doesn't
9.   Strategy changes into continuous reconfiguration
10.   Resources get trapped in the core business. Competing in arenas needs new information systems

It is difficult for companies to maintain their competitive advantage, because attractive opportunities are more visible to many more players. One can see this around one everywhere. Daily. Adapting to the ten new dimensions listed above means that companies can become more successful, because they are able to exploit temporary competitive advantage. Management should be much more challenged Where-to-Play and How-to-Win.

"Managers who are skilled at executing clearly defined strategies are ill equipped for out-of-the-box thinking and are lame ducks stuck within their comfort zone."

27. Competing in arenas needs new information systems

"It always seems impossible, until it is done", Nelson Mandela

In Section 26 we explained how crucial it is to go beyond an industry analysis towards analyses of arenas. This means it is no longer enough to look at the industry sector in which your company competes. A further step Is required, namely conducting an analysis of the 'competitive arena'.

Case example: The Port of Rotterdam
The Port of Rotterdam is Europe's largest harbor. Its traditional competitors are the harbors of Hamburg, Antwerp, Le Havre and Barcelona. However, Rotterdam is facing a very strong new competitor: Piraeus in Greece. In 2015, Piraeus was expected to have container capacity of 4.7 million TEU (in comparison, Rotterdam has a capacity of 12.0 million TEU). TEU – twenty-foot equivalent unit – is an exact measure of the capacity of container ships and container terminals. It is not the Greeks themselves, nor the EU, but the Chinese who have built this new state-of-art harbor at Piraeus. HP and Huawei are the first companies to have built terminals in Piraeus and other multinationals like Dell, IKEA, Lenovo, Samsung, and Haier are expected to follow suit. The shipping distance from Shanghai to Piraeus is 16,500 km.

The reaction of the Port of Rotterdam? Yes, we may have lost some of HP's business, but on the other hand, others will come to Rotterdam (Canon). So what? It's just a small change within one sector of the industry.

But looking at the competitive arena we see something quite different outside this sector of industry: transport by train from China to Europe and vice versa via what is being called the 'new silk route'. Transport by train means a distance of 11,000 km with an average travel time of 22 days (versus 35 days by ship). So what? Every day BMW ships containers full of spare parts by train into China. This confirms our message again that industry sector analysis is not in itself enough, and that we need analyses of competitive arenas! This is the world of strategic intelligence: to foresee change before your counterparts do so.

"We choose to go to the moon ... and do the other things, not because they are easy, but because they are hard", *John F. Kennedy in 1961*

28. **To win the strategic game**

"To win the strategic game, whether in war, chess or business, you must make a few strategic choices that will disorient your competition, so that they are unable to respond effectively"

The statement above should be common practice when we prepare ourselves to make strategic decisions. 'Strategic' is one of the most misused words in management today and is often used to mean 'important'. However, strategic decisions are about decisions with consequences of future impact for the organization. Compare this with M&A activity. Numerous research studies during the past 25 years have confirmed that 85 percent of all mergers and acquisitions fail. In the financial world, business as usual is back to where we were before the start of the 2008 crisis and it seems that Mergers & Acquisitions are back in the boardrooms. Will the same mistakes be made again with the aim of maximizing shareholder value? It looks like it.

Shareholder value versus the economic value of M&A
We are currently supporting an European company which is preparing a 'hostile' acquisition. The target company is not even aware of this.

To gain maximum success over and above simply shareholder value we apply our strategic intelligence efforts to what we call future economic drivers:

1. Beyond shareholder value: What are the future returns on investment and future risks for stakeholders apart from those who are only shareholders?
2. A deep dive in the economic drivers: what are the economic consequences and future risks for customers, employees, suppliers, the social environment and society? What is the added value for customers with better and cheaper product and service solutions and how much value will be created by destroying or creating new employment?
3. Social media: how can we develop the BARs (Before Action Reviews) related to current and future insights, assumptions and hypotheses of the potentially hostile acquisition?

This implies that our strategic intelligence efforts have to deliver strategic options away from the obvious answers, making assumptions and hypotheses away from usual routines and away from comfort zones, looking beyond one's own industry sector of towards a more complete competitive arena while avoiding future blind spots.

"To become better means change, to become perfect means to change frequently", Winston Churchill

29. The EU has a supra-national structure

"The EU has been developed to a supra-national structure carried by a spoiled, conceited and selfish euro-elite who pay little attention to what moves ordinary people", Professor Pim Fortuyn in 1997

Dutch multinationals are facing strong competitors from outside the EU, who are confronted less with the difficult market circumstances prevailing in Europe. According to research by the Dutch Financial Times FD, this concerns multinationals such as AkzoNobel, Aegon, DSM, Wolters Kluwer, KPN, Heineken and Shell. Philips and Ahold are stuck in the middle, and Reed Elsevier and Randstad are the only outperformers.

Ten years ago, ASML, Canon and Nikon were tough competitors, however ASML has since completely outmaneuvered Canon and Nikon.

In mid-April 2014, BlackRock Global Asset Management, worth some US$ 4,300 billion, gave an emerging warning to Dutch multinationals listed on the AEX Amsterdam Exchange, to invest in growth rather than in shareholder value. For example: from the total profits in 2013 of these 25 leading multinationals on the AEX, 77.3% was been paid-out to shareholders! BlackRock recommended that the boards change short-term shareholder value into long-term sustainable growth. Earlier, in February 2014, BlackRock made the same recommendations to the big corporates in the US.

We need growth
We need growth, but can we expect that growth will occur in a supra-national structured Europe? If the European population no longer believes in growth, society will slowly die. Growth is an expression of dynamics, creativity and renewal. A stagnating society chases away capital and loses confidence. Politicians look for solutions for growth such as industrial policies, the knowledge economy (Lisbon 2000), technology and innovation. We spend 35% of our income on housing, however its quality decreases with an increasing gap between the gleaming offices and residential neighborhoods. We spend 25% of our income on healthcare and education where we have been cutting costs for some 15-20 years. We spend 15% of our income on food which is still full of fat and sugar, and where obesity is becoming a huge threat to society.

Where will growth come from?
Basic occupations have to be upgraded: we need professionals who are able to build good houses and infrastructure, technicians who can run trains, strong teachers and passionate nurses. They are the builders of society. We must get rid of bureaucrats and graduates who do not contribute to society. We need practical education and schools which educate professionals, creative minds, subtle technicians and ambitious entrepreneurs.

The same choices are required in business
In a similar way to a firm's core competence of strategic intelligence and strategy, where strategic choices can be made between exploiting of one's current advantages and exploring new ones. Exploitation requires concentration on the job at hand, whereas exploration demands awareness to recognize new possibilities. If we want to make the switch from exploitation to exploration, we must make a deliberate cognitive effort to disengage from the routine to roam widely and pursue fresh paths. Although everyone has access to the same wealth of information, it is strategic intelligence that makes the difference in exploration. The challenge is to think how strategic intelligence might be applicable to you and your organization?

"A wealth of information creates a poverty of attention, and that is exactly the reason why organizations desperately need the phenomenon of strategic intelligence"

30. The corpocracy of companies

"The dream of prosperity and happiness for everybody has been disturbed by the 'corpocracy' of companies which determines everything", Professor Ewald Engelen, University of Amsterdam

The above statement is impactful and made in what I see as one of the most influential publications in Europe in 2014. We would like to share the highlights with you.

The story starts every year with the World Economic Forum in Davos, Switzerland, where the heads of the corporate world meet: CEOs, political friends and the consultancy-whisperers. They blame the politicians who are not able to solve the crisis, corporate management already has a focus on the future, and multinationals take the lead in solving the big future challenges: sustainability, growth and poverty. But five years after the largest financial crisis since the 1930s, the causes of the crisis are not still not solved: deep systemic problems remain unsolved and the welfare state is going down.

The neo-liberal utopia of privatization, liberalization and deregulation from the free market, globalization, free traffic of goods, services, capital and labor, from iPads to Starbucks, Thatcher and Reagan, from prosperity and happiness for everyone, have dropped us off and have led to huge disappointments for the majority of citizens in Western Europe. Of course, mobile devices have become cheaper, roaming is free, and we can now withdraw cash everywhere. But our income has decreased, job security is gone, healthcare and education have become worse and more expensive, democracy has been reduced, and the pressure of high taxes entangles people. Citizens got an illusion of democracy and an illusion of employee participation. The corporate world has the power to blackmail and achieved: wage moderation, less protection against dismissal, better educated labor, lower corporate taxes, more control over university research, piggy-backing on the Royal family, development cooperation in line with the corporate world, currency union, free trade agreements, less regulatory pressure, more subsidies, corporate tax deductions, places in the front row, free tickets, company names in a museum, a nearby railway station, one-on-one discussions with the Prime Minister and more. This can all be arranged, and is called 'corpocracy'. Worldwide corporate taxes have decreased by some 50% on average since the 1990s!

Corpocracy is a wonderful world
The most powerful pay the lowest taxes and the powerless pay the most taxes. In 2000, the corporate world contributed 10% to the Dutch Tax Office. In 2013 this was only 4%. The other side of the coin is that everybody else pays these taxes. Dutch multinationals such as Shell, Unilever, Philips, Heineken, ING, Rabo Bank, ABNAmro ascribe their success to our constitutional state, our legal system, our infrastructure and our education. However, the cost of maintenance is paid by the taxpayers. Who has in fact benefitted most from all of this?
Bankers, CEOs, Members of Supervisory Boards, lawyers, accountants, tax specialists and some snobbish politicians.

For the past 20 years the middle class in the US has been suffering, and for the last 10 years the situation of the middle class in Europe has been similar. Corporate savings in the Netherlands in 2014 amounted to € 60 billion. In the US this is US$ 5,000 billion.

What does the corporate world do? It doesn't invest in the domestic economies, not in research & development and not in their own employees. It still invests in shareholder value.

How then can capitalism become subservient again to the middle class?
The corporate world should think of paying decent salaries, of meeting their tax obligations, cleaning up their mess, and stopping the race to the bottom of the earth, while keeping democratic standards and values.

"If we are not able to stop the downturn of the middle class in the US and Europe, democracy will face new problems and more pressure than we have ever faced before"

31. The ventriloquists of the elite from the EU, IMF and ECB

"According to the press officers, the ventriloquists of the elite from the EU, IMF and the ECB, Greece has recovered! Please do not be so naïve as to believe this. Also blame the media, they are completely uncritical about reality"

In April 2014, many TV and radio broadcasts and publications in the media informed us that Greece had recovered. We must admit that the elite of the EU, IMF and ECB put considerable effort in the media to mislead European citizens that the Greek economy was improving. Why do they take Greece as example? Because the euro crisis started with Greece in October 2009 with the announcement that Greece was not facing a budget deficit of 3.7% but of 12.7%. However, the real figure was 15.7%. What else is the elite not telling us?

➢ The first loan in April 2010 was € 110 billion. A second loan of € 240 billion followed in March 2012
➢ In April 2014, the EU, IMF and ECB stated that Greece had a surplus of € 0.5 billion. In fact, Eurostat calculated a deficit of € 17 billion
➢ Retail sales decreased in 2013 by 8.1%
➢ Investments in 2013 were 12% of GDP (almost the lowest percentage in the world)
➢ The GDP decreased by 7% in 2013

- The total national debt, € 320 billion, is 175% of GDP
- National unemployment in 2014 was 28%
- Around 66% of young people are unemployed
- Around 1 million employed get their salaries with delays of up to 12 months
- Salaries were cut by 50% during the crisis
- 3 million people do not have access to healthcare
- 300,000 children do not have access to healthcare
- Deflation in March 2014 was 1.5%
- Since 2010, Greece's National Income decreased by 15%

Why doesn't the elite provide correct information?
The reason is simple: the European Parliamentary Elections in 2014 are the reason why Greece and the EU elite allow the Greek government to manipulate the statistics yet again. The EU wanted us to believe that they contributed to Greece's recovery by means of fierce budget cuts, privatization and liberalization. This, however, was not a solution but made the crisis worse!

Strategic intelligence
The core activity of our consultancy firm is to deliver strategic intelligence to our clients, namely delivering perspectives over and above facts. It is unthinkable to us mislead in the way the EU, IMF and ECB are regarding Greece. We hope and assume that you will stare reality straight in the eye in line with the sentiment in the statement below. It is certainly disappointing that the EU lacks leadership, vision, strategic thinking to such an extent, and suffers above all from a tremendous inability to act.

"The task of management is to stare reality straight in the eye and have the courage to act", Jack Welch

32. Contrarians are some kind of fools

"Contrarians are some kind of fools, colorful people, both loved and feared, because of their message and their stand against the obvious trends"

The majority of leaders in our organizations and in politics do not like these contrarians. However, we desperately need such people in our organizations. It is interesting to see Cesare Mainardi's research on 'losers' and 'winners' such as Amazon, Apple, IKEA, Haier, Natura and Starbucks.

One of their strengths is agility, another is being proactive. However, five 'unconventional acts' in particular make these companies both capable and successful.

The five unconventional acts are:

1. They stay true to who they are: they commit to an identity and play the strategy long game
2. They get out in front and shape what their customers want: without assiduous consumer research, but anticipating customer desires and creating demand
3. They translate their strategic intent into the everyday: they build the capabilities that matter most and execute relentlessly and flawlessly
4. They put their culture to work: they celebrate what is already great about their culture
5. They cut costs to grow stronger: they treat expenses as investments, doubling down on the capabilities that matter most in bringing value to the market

So, if you stay true to your identity, are aware of your unique strengths and where your capabilities add the most value over time, you won't only be agile, but 'smart too'.

Strategic war-gaming
To find out your organization's five unconventional acts you might consider running a strategic war game. This is a great management tool to challenge assumptions, trends and the biases of senior management. In May 2014,

we ran such a strategic war game for a Dutch multinational. The objective was to gain maximum insight, foresight and vision from four different, multidisciplinary and competitive teams, to prepare for a new product launch in an unconventional segment of the market. It is always amazing to see how much can be accomplished in just one day by using structured analysis tools such as 'five-corner analysis' and 'where-to-play' and 'how-to-win' strategy formats. At the end of the day the project director stated "why didn't we do this ten months ago?"

"Strategic intelligence is an inescapable part of every strategic decision we make in business today"

33. Only 30 percent of employees are actively committed

"Only 30% of employees are actively committed, 50% merely put time in, while the remaining 20% act in a counterproductive way, negatively influencing their co-workers and driving customers away through poor service"

What a statement! This comes from Gallup's study "State of the American Workplace 2013", published in HBR in May 2014. Is the situation any different in Europe? We think the percentages are more or less similar for Europe. How can this be changed? It is about Blue Ocean Leadership, meaning those acts and activities in which leaders are investing time and effort that should be eliminated (1), those that should be reduced well below their current level (2), those that should be raised well above the current level (3), and considerations of what acts and activities are not currently undertaken (4). It is interesting to see what activities middle and senior managers should 'raise', what they should 'create', and which are new to them.

Middle managers:

➢ 'rise' well above their current level: creating a safe environment for learning (1), explaining the strategy clearly (2), empowering frontline managers to stretch themselves (3) and coaching people (4)
➢ 'create' what they currently don't undertake: setting performance goals together (1), sharing best practices across teams (2) and aligning rewards with performance (3)

Senior managers:

➢ 'rise' well above their current level: dealing with poor performance (1), coaching and motivating direct reports (2), communicating the company's vision and what it means to people (3), creating a compelling strategy (4), and explaining the strategy clearly (5)
➢ "create" what they currently don't undertake: analyzing future trends and their implications for the company (1), developing an agenda for change (2) and removing bureaucratic blockages (3)

Blue ocean leadership confirms that senior management must take the lead in the creation of a compelling strategy as well as explaining this strategy across the company. Creating a strategy and making choices differently than key competitors are the most difficult things in management. Can senior management do this, however, since 'strategic intelligence' is missing in the majority of organizations. To briefly explain strategic intelligence: this is the difference between industry versus landscape analysis, between forecasting and foresight, between mere facts and perspectives over and above the facts, and it is about the courage to act!

Another activity, according to blue ocean leadership, that senior management should perform as a new task, is to create the means "to analyze future trends and their impact". To address this issue, we recommend to thinking beyond mere trends towards more robust Black Swans, Grey Swans, scenario planning, strategic war-mapping and 'strategy under uncertainty'.

This is where strategic intelligence makes the difference, and overcomes boardroom statements such as "Why didn't we see this coming?"

"Blue Ocean Leadership achieves a transformation with less time and effort, because leaders are not trying to alter who they are and break the habits of a lifetime"

34. Antifragility

"Antifragility at the cost of fragility of others, is hidden", Nassim Nicholas Taleb

The above statement comes from "Antifragile", by Nassim Nicholas Taleb, published in 2012. Again, this is highly-recommended, as is his 2007 book "The Black Swan". Black swans are large-scale unpredictable and irregular events that have a massive consequence. Examples are a tsunami, huge storms like Sandy in 2012, 9/11, Madrid 2004, and the loss of MH17. Antifragility means randomness, uncertainty, dealing with the unknown, doing things without understanding them and doing them well. However, it is easier to find out if something is fragile. Taleb makes the comparison with corporations: "Corporations are so fragile that they might collapse, while managers milk them for bonuses and ditch the bones to the taxpayer".

Taleb's vision of the corporate systems at corporations is critical, e.g. telecom, insurance companies, banks, healthcare sector and others:

- Corporations do not have natural ethics
- Corporations just obey the balance sheets
- The sole mission of a corporation is the satisfaction of some metrics
- Listed corporations do not feel shame
- Corporations do not feel pity
- Corporations do not have a sense of honor, while marketing documents mention 'pride'
- Corporations do not have generosity

All these defects are the result of the absence of "skin in the game", cultural or biological, an asymmetry that harms others for their own benefit. Such systems tend to implode, because ultimately one you cannot fool too many people for a too long a period of time. The problem of such an implosion is that it doesn't matter to the managers, as they will not be harmed by subsequent failures and will keep their bonuses, because there still is no such thing as negative manager's compensation.

We have recently faced too many confirming and bad examples of such corporate systems in the Netherlands and elsewhere: the return of bonuses at state-owned ABNAmro as well as at Rabo bank's Libor-gate and interest-rate derivatives and the un-professional and un-ethical behavior of tens of CEOs, Members of Supervisory Boards, Monitoring & Control Authorities and many others in the deeply rotten Dutch sector of social housing corporations. In addition, in international banking nothing has changed: it is still business as usual.

Mergers & Acquisitions are back. The sky is the limit. We have seen that large Mergers & Acquisitions are back again. We have, however, known for decades that both the poor record of M&A activities and the same managerial hubris still drive mergers, ignoring the poor economic aspects of such transactions. The economies of scale are visible, but the risks are hidden, and many concealed risks seem to bring weaknesses into the companies.

It is amazing how many special requests we regularly receive to take a 'deep dive' in troubled situations in a wide variety of organizations.

"A man is morally free when he judges the world and judges other men with uncompromising sincerity", Nassim Nicholas Taleb

35. The drama of MH17

"I didn't have the information that other airlines were behaving differently. The flight route was declared safe. The impression was that you would be safe at an altitude of 10 kilometers, however it was apparently not so because of the advanced missile systems", Camiel Eurlings, former CEO of KLM Royal Dutch Airlines

"If we should have gotten signals that the area was unsafe, then we never would have been flying there", Spokesman KLM Royal Dutch Airlines

These are merely two among many other comments relating to the dramatic flight of MH17 from Amsterdam to Kuala Lumpur. We can't blame them, we can't blame anyone, except those persons actually responsible for launching the missile on 17th July, 2014. But we can learn from this to overcome such dramatic events in the future!

Some facts:

1. On 3rd April, 2014, the US Federal Aviation Administration warned airlines not to fly over the Ukraine. This information was available to all airlines
2. On 30th June, 2014, NATO issued a warning at a press conference that the Russians were training 'separatists' in the use of advanced missile systems capable of reaching altitudes of 25 kilometers
3. Data from the UK-based "Flight Radar" shows that British Airways avoided flying over the areas of the Crimea and Ukraine. In early July 2014, the British again warned of the risks of flying over parts of Ukraine
4. The International Civil Aviation Organization ICAO, IATA and Eurocontrol gave no signs of risks about Ukraine. The Ukrainian authorities and Eurocontrol approved the MI17 flight plan
5. Security information is dealt with the Dutch Ministry of Foreign Affairs and AIVD, the Dutch Central Intelligence Service. However, the AIVD only informs airlines about their own investigations in cases where this is relevant for their aviation activities

So what can be done?

As we see in almost all cases, companies/organizations rely fully on limited sources of information and neglect to organize their own intelligence efforts. From open data – information – knowledge sources, companies and organizations are able to collect the relevant bits and pieces of the intelligence puzzle, which enables them to identify the potential risks and potential impact of future events. It is necessary to do this in every sector of industry, including the airline sector! Georgian, British, Delta, Iran, SriLankan, Vietnam and Russian UTair airlines did not fly over East-Ukraine, and passengers of UTair asked the airline to avoid East-Ukraine.

"Who delivers the crucial information on security and safe flight routes to the airlines? Is it the Aviation Authorities, Eurocontrol, IATA, ICAO, Foreign Affairs, or National Intelligence Services? Nobody in the sector really knows!"

36. Management suffers from three crucial biases

"What human beings are best at doing, is interpreting all new information so that their prior conclusions remain intact", Warren Buffett

"Too often management suffers from three crucial biases: confirmation bias, availability bias and hindsight bias. The aim of strategic intelligence is to challenge these biases and more."

We are forced to establish beliefs about the world, our lives, the economy, investments, and our careers among others. We deal mostly in assumptions, and the more indistinct these are, the stronger the confirmation bias. The 'confirmation bias' is the mother of all misconceptions: It reflects our tendency to interpret new information so that it becomes compatible with our existing theories, beliefs and convictions. We filter out any new information that contradicts our existing views. In strategic intelligence we must overcome this by delivering 'disconfirming evidence'!

Closely related to the confirmation bias is the 'availability bias'. This refers to our creating a picture of the world using those examples that come most easily to mind. Take the example of doctors: they have their favorite treatments and they tend to practice what they know. Take the example of members of the board in companies who discuss what management has submitted to them, such as the quarterly results, instead of dealing with more important issues like future scenarios, strategic risks, and potential disruptive technologies. They prefer information that is easy to obtain. Most people still overestimate Google as a source of information. In addition, people prefer incorrect information to no information! Strategic intelligence delivers perspectives based on facts.

A third bias, which is closely related to the confirmation and availability biases, is the 'hindsight bias'. In 2007, financial 'experts' painted a rosy picture for the coming years. However, in the fall of 2008 the financial markets imploded. Those same experts then explained the causes to us, namely Greenspan's monetary expansion policy, rotten mortgages, corrupt rating-agencies, too low capital requirements at banks, and so on. In hindsight, the reasons for the financial crisis seem painfully obvious. Strategic intelligence is about creating better insight and future-based foresight based on pre-events, the timely identification of Grey Swans, and scenario planning.

If you wish to learn much more you might consider attending our two-day international master class on strategic intelligence, scheduled twice per year in the Netherlands, which is recognized in Europe as the leading training course in strategic intelligence.

"The availability bias caused banks to lose billions from 2007 to 2009. However, the key problem is that it is still 'business as usual' at those same banks"

37. **We didn't see it**

"We didn't foresee the fall in investment in our industrial sector"

This statement by Paul van Riel, CEO of Fugro, in the Dutch financial newspaper Het Financieele Dagblad on 30th October, 2014. Fugro is the world's largest integrator of geotechnical survey, subsea and geosciences services. The company is 70-80 percent dependent on what is going on in the oil and gas sector. In September 2013, Fugro launched its new "Growth through Leadership" strategy aimed at an annual growth of 10 percent in the next couple of years. In the spring of 2014, the first warnings were issued regarding under-performance and pressure on profitability.

Difficult to imagine
In November 2014, just two months after Fugro's new strategy launch, French Total decreased its investment plans and other major key players in the sector followed suit. How is it possible that they didn't foresee this basic change? Fugro's new strategy was apparently not based on strategic intelligence, deepening the insights and foresight of their sector of industry and beyond, towards the complete dynamics regarding the future competitive landscape. It is clear that Fugro did not have an early warning system in place.

In developing a strategy there are two directions: strategy as a resource-allocation process laced with pride, or strategy as insight and foresight generation. In the first, the process of resource allocation is in most cases politically protected by senior management, and is not what is most valuable for the company. You might see this as strategy development within one's comfort zone with a focus on costs. However, strategy development driven by strategic intelligence is always outside one's comfort zone: it is based on revenues not costs, your beliefs about your customers, beyond the limited scope of analysis of the sector of industry towards getting the insights and foresight for the future competitive landscape, and fine-tuning your own capabilities which give the necessary answers during strategy development: 'Where-to-Play' and 'How-to-Win'.

Strategic intelligence and strategy tools for the years ahead
To create the real insights and foresight in the future-driven competitive landscape consider the following strategic intelligence and strategy tools: scenario planning and analysis, strategic war-mapping for future courses of action, strategy under uncertainty, strategy as active waiting, where-to-play/how-to-win and early warning as result of 24/7 active monitoring. These tools can be used in combination, aiming to achieve maximum results. These tools allow you to start with strategy development outside your comfort zone, and this is how you can get to the heart of strategic intelligence.

"The more highly-paid the directors who you put on your board, the more handsomely they are likely to reward you", Freek Vermeulen

38. Contextual intelligence

"International executives need 'contextual intelligence', the ability to recognize the limits of their knowledge and adapt it to different environments"

The statement above was made by Tarun Khanna in Harvard Business Review in both September and November 2014. Context is the background in which a future event takes place, it is often real or perceived and includes factors such as geography, genders, industries, job roles, attitudes, beliefs, values, politics, cultures, symbols, organizational climate, the past, personal ethics and the preferred future. Intelligence is the ability to transform data into useful information, information into knowledge, and knowledge into intelligence. Contextual intelligence is a leadership competency and can be learned and used by any person, in any place, at any time. Contextually intelligent people have the perfect intuition of knowing how to ask the right questions, at the right time, to the right people.

Contextually intelligence-based questions include:

1. Whose responsibility is this?
2. How does this influence the anticipated or desired future?
3. Who determines what is and what is not a success?
4. Who has the power and how do they control information?
5. Who is supposed to make this decision versus who actually makes this decision?
6. Who are the recognized leaders?
7. Who are the unrecognized leaders?
8. Who are the followers and who do they follow?
9. What roles need to be accomplished to get this done?
10. What experiences can I relate to this?
11. Whose experiences can I relate to this?
12. What historical events led to this situation or required decision?

For practitioners in strategic competitive intelligence and strategy this means having the ability to recognize, assess and assimilate the various internal and external factors inherent in a given environment or circumstance by interpreting and by reacting appropriately to rapidly-changing surroundings. This separates leaders from non-leaders. Leaders who are multi-tasking thinkers who routinely go outside their comfort zones to acquire useful intelligence about the world in which they live, work and integrate this intelligence into their decision-making.

"The secret of getting ahead is getting started. The secret of getting started is breaking your complex overwhelming tasks into small manageable ones, and then starting on the first one"

39. Top management and change

"Why doesn't top management see change?"

We frequently ask ourselves "Why doesn't top management see change?" In 2014, the Dutch financial newspaper, Het Financieele Dagblad, published an astonishing article about another international Dutch company taken by surprise: SBM Offshore. This company is active in the global offshore oil & gas exploration business. The newspaper heading was "Market forces us to lay off jobs". SBM Offshore had to fire 1,200 out of a workforce of 10,000 people. It was stated that "we anticipate the developments in the oil & gas sector". But this is incorrect! SBM Offshore didn't anticipate, they reacted to changes in the market, which they already could have foreseen 12 months previously.

SBM Offshore does not apparently have a corporate radar. Together with many other companies SBM Offshore operates in a VUCA (Volatile, Uncertain, Complex, and Ambiguous) world. VUCA has never been more relevant in the military as well as in the business sector. Strategic intelligence professionals are able to "to see around corners" and are able to see something significant about the future that others and thus top management don't see. Strategic intelligence supports top management in what they want to accomplish, so that the company can better execute its business in the volatility, uncertainty, complexity, and ambiguity of today's global business environment.

84

"I do not believe you can do today's job with yesterday's methods and be in business tomorrow"

40. Management and strategic choices

"Management can never be completely comfortable with its strategic choices because the company is then at risk of missing the dynamics of change in their business environment"

The statement above is about strategy, the most difficult topic in business today. Strategy is not about vision-mission-objectives-strategies.
Neither is it the descriptive front-end of the yearly budget as we see too often. It is also not about costs, which are under the control of management. Strategy is about making choices differently from the competition and about revenues, whereby it is the customer who is in charge and not the management! Strategic intelligence is the precondition to becoming successful in creating unique strategies. Why? Because this is not about prediction or unrealistic and wishful forecasting, but because strategic intelligence delivers the ultimate insights and foresight for strategy.

On 24-25 February, 2015, the international pharmaceutical industry gathered in Amsterdam on the topic of competitive intelligence. The sector shared their expertise and experiences amongst 175 delegates from international companies such as Abbott, AstraZeneca, Bayer, Biogen, Boehringer Ingelheim, Celgene, Chiesi, Daiichi Sankyo, Debiopharm, Fresenius, Helsinn, Janssen Pharma, Merck, MSD, Novartis, Novo Nordisk, Roche, Sanofi, Sanofi-Aventis, Shire Pharmaceuticals, Takeda, Teva, Zambon and others. It was an honor for our firm to give the keynote opening speech at this European conference. Why was it so interesting to attend this conference? Simply, because pharma is well ahead of the game in competitive intelligence. It was also amazing to note that only two out of the 175 participants were from the Netherlands and Belgium.

"It Can't Be True"
This is the title of the book by Joris Luyendijk, who did in-depth research for 2 years in the City of London. His conclusion: nothing has changed since 2008. The complete structure of the status-driven financial sector in the

City is focused only on earning as much money as possible. Everyone is fighting everyone to get as much out of the 'bonus pool' as they can. In February 2015, € 123 billion in bonuses were paid in the City alone! The situation in 2015 is exactly the same as in 2008. In the next section we will examine this in more detail.

"Consensus is good, unless it is achieved too easily, in which case it becomes suspect"

41. Highlights from "It Can't Be True"

"Imagine you sit in an airplane, relaxing with a glass of wine, and when looking out of the window you see the engine is on fire. There is no cabin crew. In the chaos you make your way to the front of the plane and open the door of the cockpit only to find that there are no pilots"

This is how research journalist Joris Luyendijk describes the current situation in the financial sector in his book "It Can't Be True". Nothing has changed since the start of the crisis in 2008!

"It Can't Be True"
The book, published in February 2015, was based on 2 years of research from over 200 in-depth interviews in the City of London. In his book. Luyendijk makes comparisons with the world of animals: traders are baboons, investment bankers are tigers, back-office employees are hard-working beavers and the departments of compliance and risk management are ants. The majority of the employees in the sector are therefore beavers and ants whose task is to control the tigers and baboons. Mission impossible!

One crucial conclusion is that the entire structure of the social status focused financial sector is driven by trying to earn as much as possible. Every year banks dismiss some of their worst-performing employees in addition to regular layoffs and cost-cutting. In this environment, it is take what you can for as long as you can. Everyone fights everyone else to try and get their share of the bonus pool. Long-term solidarity and good fellowship are seen as handicaps.

Since the start of the crisis in 2008 nothing has changed and the main culprits of the crisis are the traders and investment bankers.

What about the Dutch banks ING, ABNAmro and Rabobank?
The situation in the City isn't fundamentally different from that at the three major banks in the Netherlands. Research from the Dutch newspaper NRC (14 March, 2015) showed that ING, ABNAmro and Rabobank wrote off € 30 billion in 'bad loans' since the 2008 crisis. They recovered from this huge loss by decreasing interest rates on savings and increasing the interest rates on credit. The banks made provisions for 'expected problems' on potential problems with loans but not for 'unexpected problems' such as Grexit and the related crisis in the euro-system. For the financial sector, Grexit is a Grey Swan, not least because the levels of equity at these banks show up on their balance sheets as 5-6% on average, on total assets which are far too low.

In Section 20, we discussed the vision of Anat Admati, Professor of Economics at Stanford's Graduate School of Finance, who stated that the requirement of equity at banks needs to increase to 20-30 percent of total assets! Banks still argue that economic growth will suffer, but they should ask themselves why Europe is still in crisis since 2008. If banks become smaller, it should be easier to get new capital. Banks are too large, inefficient, difficult to manage and difficult to regulate.

At Rodenberg Tillman & Associates, we are optimistic and a little paranoid by nature, because we are active in strategic intelligence. However, after reading "It Can't Be True", we are not positive about the future of banks. We expect that the 'millennials' will break down the banks in the end, so that one of my statements in my first book on competitive intelligence (published in 2000) will come true: "banking is necessary, banks are not".

"It's insane that banks still pay dividends to shareholders. By doing this, capital is flowing out, it should, however, be used to strengthen their own equity", Professor Anat Admati

42. The balance sheets of the big banks are black holes

"The balance sheets of the big banks are the blackest of all black holes",
Andrew Haldane, Chief Economist, Bank of England

We generally never deal with the same topic three times in a row. But in this case we have to, because there is so much wrong in the financial sector. What do you think about the above quote from the Bank of England's Chief Economist, listed by TIME Magazine as being in the Top-100 most influential people in the world? To us this of great concern, though most people in the world don't realize it.

Our latest insights come from research journalist Joris Luyendijk book "It Can't Be True".

Here is his list of the top-10 most remarkable insights:

1.   There is deep mutual distrust in the middle of an amoral focus on profit and revenue responsibility
2.   If you are under such huge pressure and will never be seen as legally responsible, then why, as a banker, should you not 'screw' a client
3.   Top management at both US and UK banks didn't have a clue where the profits came from, nor what the risks were
4.   Standard & Poor's, Fitch and Moody's valued CDOs and their complex spin-offs as 'super save' and 'triple-A'. Why didn't the accountants or board of directors see this or tell us?
5.   Standard & Poor's, Fitch and Moody's are paid by the banks, and yet they judge the banks' financial products as though they are 'independent'. This is similar to the inspectors of the Michelin Guide not tasting anonymously and being paid by the chefs they are evaluating
6.   The top management of the banks does not know what is going on, because the banks are too large and too complex
7.   If you had suggested at the peak of the crisis, that after the crisis no fundamental reforms would have been executed, no one would have believed you

8. In addition to being 'too big to fail', there are also 'too big to save' and 'too big to manage'
9. Banks are still not transparent and never have taken formal leave from bankers who put the bank's reputation at risk, neither the accounting firms and neither the credit-rating agencies. On the contrary, banks invested heavily in the lobby against the increase of the capital requirements
10. In the financial world, the 'code of silence' still rules the sector

"The next crash will hurt us extremely badly. The banks in Brussels, Amsterdam and in other capitals are just branch offices of the City and Wall Street. No government in the world has any control nor will they gain control in the years to come"

43. Companies do not exist for ever

"Why don't companies last forever? Why do so many companies face serious problems after years of success? Why does management not react if the success rate of organizations comes to an end?"

This is because your company's internal business intelligence dashboards, your big-data analytics, and the managers with titles like market insights, customer insights, marketing intelligence and market intelligence do not deliver the right intelligence!

We are right, aren't we? Think of companies like GM, Nokia, Blackberry, HP, Panasonic, Sharp, Sony, Getronics, Air France-KLM, Alstom, banks in Europe and elsewhere? Or the following companies in the Netherlands: Hans Textiel, Piet Kerkhof, Henk ten Hoor, Schoenenreus, Scapino, Free Record Shop, Marlies Dekkers, OAD, Halfords, Koops Automotive, Mexx, V&D, Imtech, MacIntosh, Vion Food Group, Van Gansewinkel and Ballast Nedam. All these companies have been in deep trouble and only a few have survived. Why is this?

We know why this happens, but we don't act.
The key reason why these companies and so many others run into deep trouble is because they do not adapt in time to discontinuous change. And

although we all know that discontinuous changes come from outside our companies, we continue to make the mistake of looking mainly inside. Strategic intelligence can help foresee in good time (at least 12-18 months ahead) whether the company is facing a strategic crisis. The mother of all strategic crises is the loss of competitive advantage. The challenge faced by strategic intelligence professionals is to deliver strategic intelligence which cannot be ignored, taking into account the high rate of future change, and overcoming ignorance and inertia.

What should companies do?
Companies have to take a step ahead by moving from level 1-2 towards level 3-4 on what we call the Intelligence Continuum. Levels 1-2 are about data and information and Levels 3-4 are about intelligence.

Level 1:   Competitive data collection: focus on market, customer and channel information – tactical
Level 2:   Industry and competitive analysis: focus on current markets and competitors – tactical
Level 3:   Competitive intelligence: focus on understanding the industry, technology, customers, competitors and legislation – tactical/strategic
Level 4:   Strategic intelligence: this covers a broad range of topics of strategic significance, strategic crisis, Grey Swans, and future competitive landscape

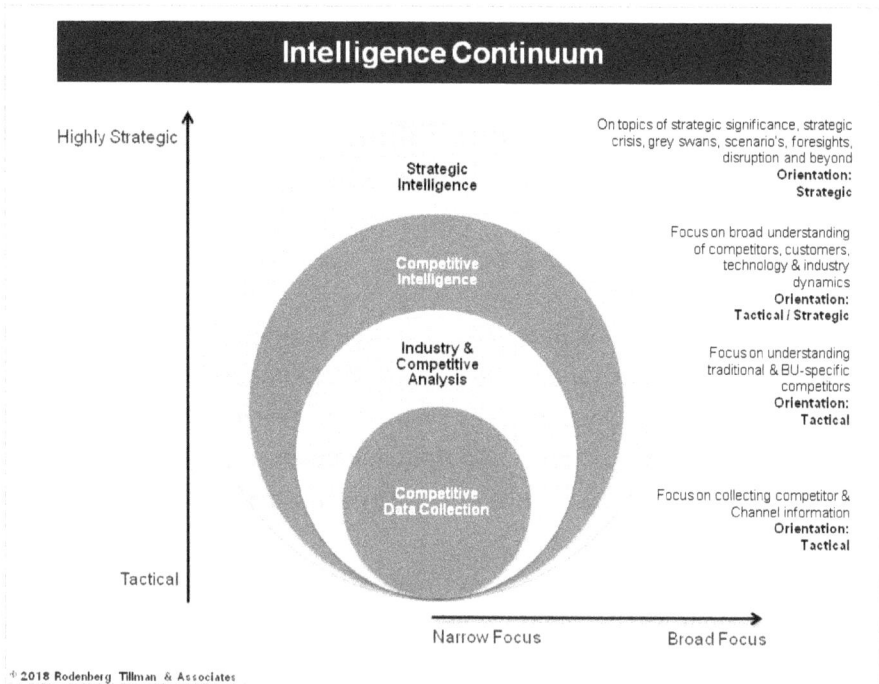

Intelligence Continuum

Highly Strategic

Strategic Intelligence — On topics of strategic significance, strategic crisis, grey swans, scenario's, foresights, disruption and beyond
Orientation: Strategic

Competitive Intelligence — Focus on broad understanding of competitors, customers, technology & industry dynamics
Orientation: Tactical / Strategic

Industry & Competitive Analysis — Focus on understanding traditional & BU-specific competitors
Orientation: Tactical

Competitive Data Collection — Focus on collecting competitor & Channel information
Orientation: Tactical

Tactical

Narrow Focus — Broad Focus

© 2018 Rodenberg Tillman & Associates

What we can see is that most organizations find it difficult to leave Levels 1-2 behind, because they are stuck in day-to-day operations within their business units or divisions. In addition, managers in these organizations struggle to get out of their comfort zones and continue managing their businesses as usual. This is why so many companies do not foresee discontinuous changes in the external business environment in a timely manner. In the next section, we consider how to do this.

"Strategic intelligence is unequalled intelligence presented to top management that cannot be ignored"

44. Intelligence is externally driven

"If intelligence is not driven externally, then one is not doing intelligence"

"If a company is interested in finding the future, most of what it needs to do is to learn from outside the industry sector", Gary Hamel

91

In the previous section we discussed a wide variety of some twenty-five companies that lost momentum because they failed to react in a timely fashion to discontinuous changes in their external business development. We described why this happens to so many companies and what can be done to overcome this. Here we explain how to do this.

We recommend four courses of action:

1. Scenario planning: determine what the potential Grey Swans will be 5-8 years ahead, and which of these might impact the existence of the company. Once the Grey Swans have been identified, determine the variables of potential influence. Then start creating your strategic intelligence efforts to generate the levels of uncertainty – impact

2. Strategic War-Mapping: determine where current and potential/new competitors might hurt your company. Get into the mind of your rivals and also think the unthinkable. The time scope is to be 12-36 months ahead of the game in the current and future competitive arena

3. Company Radar Room: This is where the variables which influence the Grey Swans in general and more specifically those which influence future changes in the market, customers, competitors, legislation and technology, are monitored 24/7. The big challenge of your strategic intelligence efforts is to create 'early warnings' for top management. This generates maximum insight and foresight regarding the main issues for long-term company survival

4. Four-Corner Analysis on your competitor's Future Strategy: the focus here is on your key competitors conducting an analysis on their current strategy (1), competitors' capabilities (2), elements driving the financials, management style, leadership, constraints and culture (3) and finally elements to identify perceptions, expectations, foresight and imagination (4)

Creating these four courses of action means that you will be in a position to deliver 'actionable strategic intelligence' that cannot be ignored by top management. Intelligence that cannot be ignored does not come from databases, IT-systems, big data or from the internet. It is, however, the result of analysis as the key to actionable intelligence. Intelligence is created only by analysts. This implies that the strategic intelligence team works continuously and consistently on all the factors, elements, drivers and variables of these four courses of action for the future.

"The truest characters of ignorance are vanity, pride and arrogance"

45. **The agile company**

"To become an agile company means gaining the ability to see both opportunities and threats and then executing the strategies needed to address them"

Strategic intelligence enables top management to foresee the opportunities and threats in a timely fashion. At the end of the day who is accountable? Being agile as a company depends on developing two key capabilities: responsiveness and organizational flexibility. Many of us see new business opportunities. However, most of us are concerned that our companies lack the skills needed to meet future competitive threats. But it is not just competition, rather competitiveness, that counts. Strategic responsiveness is the ability to sense new risks and new opportunities in the business environment and craft a quick response to those pressures. Organizational flexibility is the ability to shift execution rapidly.
Companies face these challenges, but what about countries? Our banks, governments and the media tell us that Europe is 'out of crisis', performing with low growth rates of 0.5 to 2.0 percent. Concerning strategic responsiveness and organizational flexibility, it will be interesting to look at the EU's competitiveness and not limit ourselves merely to the EU's internal market.

The 2015 IMD World Competitiveness Scoreboard of 60 countries showed two key trends:

Countries which lost competitiveness: Germany, France, UK, Sweden, Finland, Netherlands, Austria, Estonia, Latvia, Slovakia, Romania, Bulgaria and Hungary;

Countries which gained competitiveness: Denmark, Norway, Belgium, Lithuania, Czech Republic, Poland and the southern European countries Portugal, Spain, Italy and even Greece.

According to the IMD, productivity and efficiency are in the driver's seat of competitiveness. Business efficiency requires greater productivity, and the competitiveness of countries is greatly linked to the ability of companies to remain profitable over time. Increasing productivity remains a fundamental challenge for all countries. But here we face another problem: gains in productivity are about the long term and not the short term.

"Strategic intelligence enables top management to increase future competitiveness, whereby strategic intelligence serves, in effect, as the CEO's Chief of Staff"

46. Trust never returns

"I have learned in life that in contacts with people there is no alternative to trust. Trust comes slowly and leaves quickly and never returns to the place it has left."

The statement is one of my favorites. Trust in society is under huge pressure. We can see some extremely negative developments which are out of the control of our politicians, who unfortunately do not have the courage to take the necessary tough decisions.
Leadership is lacking in Europe. For one of our clients, we have been active in navigating and facilitating a scenario-planning process towards 2025. This is a difficult path of potential actions because "scenario planning is not just a study of the future, but of the future success of decisions taken today". During the scenario-planning process, we faced some Black Swans as well as Grey Swans, which could potentially harm the organization.

Below we list some Grey Swans:

1. The shrinking middle class in the US, Europe and Japan. The implication: less spending by the middle class which will hurt the multinational companies in the long term

2. Money printing by the FED, ECB and the Central Bank in Japan. In the financial world this is called QE, Quantitative Easing. The implication: shifting our growing debts to future generations
3. The euro might implode. During the past few hundred years there have been tens of monetary unions, all of which have imploded. The implication: Greece will leave and other countries may follow
4. The EU doesn't deliver. Weak leadership makes the EU a "fighting union" unable to protect the middle class. The implications: sharing prosperity is getting out-of-balance, with increasing aging, less safety and security, and growing flows of refugees
5. Social cohesion in Europe. People have lost their beliefs in a united Europe. The implications: limited investment and weak job creation. More disruption is desired to increase the future competitiveness of Europe
6. Investments are under pressure. Companies are piling up cash despite low interest rates, households are reluctant to spend following the crisis in 2008. The implications: a collectively weakening in demand, resulting in 8-12% less output compared to the years before the crisis

According to McKinsey, European countries need to take three paths to change the current baseline growth of 0-1% to a new potential growth of 2-3% towards 2025: investing for the future (1), boosting productivity (2) and mobilizing the workforce (3). In the previous section, the 2015 IMD report on competitiveness confirmed that one of the key drivers to strengthen future competitiveness is to increase productivity.

"The only relevant questions about the future are those where we succeed from shifting the question from whether something will happen to 'what we would do if it did happen'"

47. Quantitative Easing by the FED and ECB

"How long will this last with zero interest rates politics, quantitative easing by the FED and ECB, and fast-growing debts around the world?"

A short story: "It is July 2015 on the shores of the Mediterranean. Times are tough, everyone is in debt and everyone lives on credit. Suddenly a rich tourist comes to town; he enters a hotel and puts a € 100 note on the reception counter to inspect some of the upstairs rooms for that evening. The hotel owner takes the € 100 note and runs to the butcher to pay his debt. The butcher takes the € 100 note and runs to the supplier of feed and fuel to pay his debt. The supplier takes the € 100 note and runs to the town's prostitute to pay-off his credit. The hooker runs to the hotel and pays off her debt with the € 100 note for the rooms she rented. The hotel owner puts the € 100 note back on the counter so that the rich tourist will not suspect anything.

The tourist comes down after inspecting the rooms and takes the € 100 note, because he didn't like the rooms, and leaves town."

The bottom line: no one earned anything, but the whole town is now without debt and looks to the future with increased optimism.

Use your imagination: China might collapse like a house of cards and the US might face a new recession. Financial markets are driven by bubbles and the economy gives delusionary hope. Central banks lose control and we can expect more chaotic developments in the financial markets. Are those of us, active in strategic intelligence, pessimistic or realistic by bringing you face-to-face you with several macro-economic Grey Swans? Please give this some future perspective some thought.

"How is strategy developed in your organization? Is strategy a resource-allocation process or is it an insights and foresight generation process?"

48. Ordinary and Dynamic Capabilities

"A clear strategic direction is a concise set of choices that determines what we do and what we don't do", Freek Vermeulen

Many years ago, Michael Porter said that strategy is about making choices differently from your rivals. It is interesting to make the connection with Professor David Teece of the University of California at Berkeley, regarding 'dynamic capabilities', the internal company drivers of strategy that point towards competitive positioning. Teece draws a distinction between ordinary and dynamic capabilities. Ordinary capabilities are a set of learned processes and activities that enable a company to produce a particular outcome and are similar to best practices. Automobile companies may know how to build an assembly line but it still took most of them more than 25 years to learn the 'Toyota Way'. This means automobile companies are no longer unique. Dynamic capabilities are those capabilities unique to each company and are rooted in the company's history, not just in routines but in business models that go back decades and are difficult to imitate, as implied for example, in the response "This is the way things are done around here".

Three types of managerial activities make a capability dynamic:

1. Sensing: identifying and assessing opportunities outside your company
2. Seizing: mobilizing your resources to capture value from those opportunities
3. Transforming: continuous renewal

This is about how to get to the future in an optimum way, about how to position today's resources properly for tomorrow. Compare Nokia with Apple; Nokia missed the smartphone revolution because it was not well equipped for sensing. Nokia tapped heavily into the science and technology, but missed the prevailing state of mind. We can see how important competitive intelligence is because we know that one of the core objectives of competitive intelligence is to 'sense' what is going on in the external business environment and how future dynamics can impact the company. Can we learn from this? Yes, even more because this is the difference between traditional competitive intelligence with a short- to mid-term perspective versus strategic intelligence which has a mid- to long-term view.

"Culture eats strategy for breakfast", Peter Drucker

49. Too often the Egos of CEOS are too Big

"Adjusting a company in the midst of the whirlwind of decline is like trying to turn a tanker around in an iceberg field", Trojan Horses of Decline

In 2015, a high-technological corporation in the Netherlands, Royal Imtech, with some 22,000 employees, active in infrastructure, building & construction, maintenance & control, ran into financial trouble. The main causes of this bankruptcy were the inflated egos of the former CEO and CFO, who had both held positions from 2002 till February 2013, acting like 'sun-kings', and a lack of monitoring and control. The company's headquarters had no idea what was happening in the divisions and in the subsidiaries: the numerous acquisitions made from 2002 to 2012 all kept their own ICT-systems as well as their own finance & administration systems.

Former top management was driven by growth by means of acquisitions: € 1.5 billion in 2002, € 5 billion in 2015 and an aim of € 8 billion in 2020. Only one analyst at ABNAmro began asking critical questions in fall of 2012, but the 'messenger was shot'. Nobody at all, whether analysts at banks, unions, or institutes like the Authority Financial Markets, or the Dutch Central Bank and others were critical. In December 2012, the Dutch financial world had their yearly party in Amsterdam to choose the best M&A director, the best M&A advisor, the best M&A banker and another "24 best in ……. Functions". At this party Royal Imtech's CFO was chosen as the best director in M&A. Yet just four weeks later he was forced to resign due to extreme bad governance, fraud and many other failures.

Strategic intelligence

The only way to create the necessary countervailing power to top management, boards of management and boards of directors, is to establish the office of Strategic Intelligence on a par with other functions that report directly to senior management.

"Strategic Intelligence prevents top management of looking like fools a few years down the road"

50. Big Boys Big Ego's and Strategic Intelligence

"There are only three reasons why companies get into trouble: big boys ego's, outdated strategies and a lack of both inside and outside"

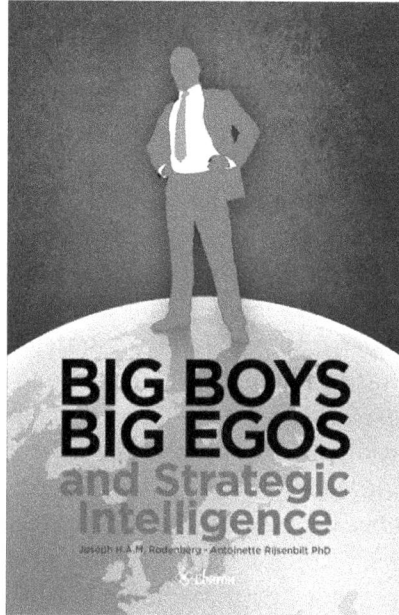

BIG BOYS BIG EGOS and Strategic Intelligence

Joseph H.A.M. Rodenberg - Antoinette Rijsenbilt PhD

In the fall of 2015, we published our book "Big Boys Big Egos and Strategic Intelligence", the fifth book in a row on business-, competitive- and strategic intelligence since 2000. Scientific research on narcissism lies at the basis of this book, which is based on a sample of 950 CEOs of the S&P top-500 companies during the period 1992-2009. The narcissism construct is measured using a massive dataset regarding CEO media exposure, compensation, power, growth and perquisites. From these five core elements, fifteen determinants were identified which made it possible to measure the level of narcissism objectively. These include: the number of mentions in the press, number of awards, size of photographs in the annual report, remuneration, duality in the top role, number and size of acquisitions, and private use of the corporate jet. Narcissism can be productive and destructive.

Examples of leaders exhibiting productive narcissism are Steve Jobs (Apple), Michael Eisner (Walt Disney), Jack Welch (GE), Ingvard Kampard (IKEA) and Henry Ford (Ford Motor Company). They are all leaders with vision and charisma who were able to inspire and motivate their employees. Examples of leaders demonstrating destructive narcissism are the 'sun-kings' at the top of the public and private sector as well as in politics.

Strategic intelligence

Our research shows that strategic intelligence is the way to create countervailing power towards the board of management and board of directors. A small team of 3-4 strategic intelligence professionals are perfectly able to do this, positioned beyond risk management, with the aim of creating the maximum future-based insights and foresight related to all the crucial elements in the dynamics of change in the company's external environment. A key objective is act in a timely manner to prevent situations in which the company might face a strategic crisis. The strategic intelligence team uses uncommon analysis tools to generate these future-based insights and foresight: strategic war-mapping, scenario analysis, competitive arena analysis, Grey Swan analysis, strategy under uncertainty and early warning. In addition, they have at their disposal a radar room which supports them in constantly monitoring the external environment. This allows the team to generate countervailing power towards top management and prevent board members looking like fools a few years down the road.

"Strategic Intelligence prevents top management of looking like fools a few years down the road"

51. We live in a VUCA world

"A wealth of information creates a poverty of attention", economist Herbert Simon, 1971. That is why strategic intelligence is needed to get the necessary insights and foresight and make better decisions!

If you are dissatisfied with strategy-making based on information, backward-looking analysis, management controls and problem-solving after the event, but you would still like to make a positive contribution to thinking about the future, it is time for strategic intelligence.

This implies moving from the basics of data and information gathering for industry analysis to competitive intelligence towards strategic intelligence.

Strategic intelligence helps determine the most important dangers for your business and minimize their impact if they materialize. Organizations have never had a greater need for a flexible, resilient and engaging approach to strategic intelligence than now. Think of our business world whereby, VUCA sets the stage for managing and leading companies on the right course of action.

- Many thousands of companies can make better decisions in the event that they have strategic intelligence in place
- Strategic intelligence is the way to organize the countervailing power to senior management as described in "Big Boys Big Ego's and Strategic Intelligence" (published in October 2015)
- In Strategic Intelligence we use unique tools such as Strategic War-Mapping, PARTS, SPACE, Grey Swan analysis, SWOTI 2.0 and others
- VUCA stands for Volatility, Uncertainty, Complexity and Ambiguity. For leaders both in the military and in business, this approach underscores the importance of strategic decision-making, readiness planning, risk management and situational problem-solving.

In a VUCA world, top management faces challenges of new customer needs, increased competition, disruptive innovation, a rapidly-changing competitive arena, currency volatility, financial instability and worse, cybersecurity, volatility in energy markets, activist shareholders, new government regulations, bribery, corruption and much more. Strategic intelligence delivers the vision to better anticipate and react to the nature and speed of change (1), creates foresight to act decisively in uncertain situations (2), delivers system thinking to navigate the organization through complexity, chaos, confusion and worse (3). Strategic intelligence is executed by a small core team that gives top management the necessary countervailing power with the aim of preventing mismanagement a few years down the road.

"Strategic Intelligence is executed by a small team supported by a Company Radar Room"

52. Book summary - Big Boys Big Ego's and Strategic Intelligence

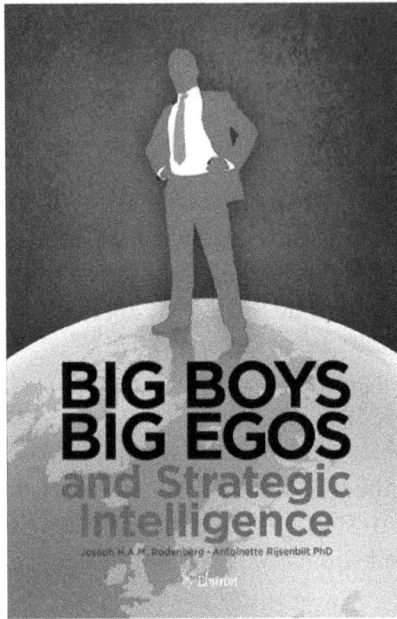

Strategic intelligence creates the countervailing power towards destructive narcissism of the Big Egos

Narcissism is widespread at the top in both private and public companies as well as in non-profit organizations and the public sector. Narcissism is a necessary element for effective leadership, but it can, however, also become a negative trait. So we may therefore speak about positive and destructive narcissism. Examples to be emulated are Steve Jobs (Apple), Michael Eisner (Walt Disney), Jack Welch (GE), Ingvard Kamprad (IKEA), Henri Ford (Ford Motor Company), Freddie Heineken (Heineken) and Richard Branson (Virgin). All are leaders with vision and charisma who have been able to inspire and motivate their employees tremendously. But there are also examples of destructive narcissism; think of the 'sun-kings' at the top of many private and public companies and in politics. Examples include top management at banks, insurance companies, NGOs, public organizations, and Sepp Blatter (FIFA) and Michel Platini (UEFA) in sport. Research shows that narcissism can be measured objectively by looking at five key elements which tell us something about the narcissistic personality of the CEO. These five elements are media, remuneration, power, growth and emoluments.

Variables which we can objectively determine include, amongst others, the number of publications in the press, number of awards, size of photo(s) in the annual report, compensation, duality, number and size of acquisitions and special perquisites such as private use of the corporate jet. Narcissism is not necessarily a personality disorder, but can be expressed on a scale on which one may score either high or low.

Strategic intelligence is the way to organize countervailing power towards the board of management and the board of directors. Strategic intelligence is executed by a small team of 3-4 professionals who report directly to the board. This means that strategic intelligence is positioned at the highest level in the organization, above risk management, because the focus of strategic intelligence is on gaining maximum insight and foresight on all aspects of the dynamics of change in the external business environment: future developments of markets, customers, competition, new legislation, and new technologies. The key objective of strategic intelligence is to try and prevent in a timely way a situation where the company faces a strategic crisis, and thereby avoid the usual solutions of cost-cutting and personnel layoffs. In addition to delivering the necessary countervailing power to the big egos, the strategic intelligence team counteracts arrogance and complacency at the top, preventing the company from relying too much on past successes.

The Ford Motor Company shows a nice example of how to do this. When Alan Mulally moved from being CEO at Boeing to become CEO of Ford in 2006, he initiated a policy of cost-cutting and debt reduction. In 2009 Ford returned to profit after the heavy losses of US$ 14.7 billion in 2006. What made the crucial difference? When Mulally started at Ford he created a strategic intelligence team with a war room, in which he had three walls each with a different color: green, orange, and red. This was Mulally's strategic intelligence approach to visualize 'Ford's Global Battlefield' and his way of structuring the countervailing power at the top of the company.

Air France-KLM is a company where countervailing towards the board of management and board of directors failed. In 2004, KLM was sold to Air France. For many years KLM suffered from Air France's under-performance and from fierce competition from easyJet and Ryanair. Ryanair even considered starting using Amsterdam Schiphol Airport, KLM's home base, in 2016.

At the end of the 1990s Ryanair started competing on price as price: In 2000 they had just 13 planes (KLM had 186), in 2005 they had 60 planes (KLM 182) and in 2015, 320 planes (KLM 200).

Other examples of destructive narcissism are the disasters of the 'Sun-Kings' at the Dutch housing corporation sector, at Royal Imtech, and at Volkswagen in 2016.

Strategic intelligence professionals use unique analysis tools such as strategic war-mapping, scenario analysis, competitive arena analysis and Grey Swan analysis, strategy under uncertainty, and early warning. Strategic intelligence professionals deliver actionable intelligence to top management to help them make the best decisions, 12-24 months ahead of the game. This is their way to give countervailing power to those at the top. These professionals are able to do so because they have at their disposal a Company Radar Room whereby all the dynamics of change in the external business environment are constantly monitored. In addition to Ford Motor Company, another excellent example of a company which has a radar room or war room in place is Cisco.

53. Everything can be digitized

"Everything that can be digitized will reduce value and everything that can't be digitized will increase value", Salim Ismail, Founder of Singularity University

The digital revolution is underway with the biggest hotel chain Airbnb that doesn't even own a single hotel room, and Uber, the biggest taxi-company that doesn't even own a single car. The value-chain as we know it will change and be replaced by service-offering systems. This has already happened with the telecom, travel and music sectors. During the next 10 years some 70% of jobs will disappear! For organizations, this means disruptive change requiring more flexibility, different ways of working without hierarchical structures, and the ability to organize in small flexible units. This will give companies the opportunity to innovate and to scale-up rapidly. Even Google recognized that it had to change, and did so by restructuring and establishing Alphabet, their new holding company. We changed our strategic intelligence practices some years ago by using many more 'pre-decision-making analysis tools' such as strategy by uncertainty, strategic war-mapping, scenario analysis, Grey Swan analysis, current market place and future space analysis, and analysis of constraints.

This resulted in much better insight and foresight because it enabled organizations to identify the crucial Key Predictive Indicators of future change in a timely way.

Indicators of constraints

The key question is, whether this replacement by service-offering systems is going to happen during the next downturn of the world economy. Some indicators of constraints include the following: first we had the US with the bursting of the housing bubble, then Europe with the financial, euro and economic crisis and now the upcoming crisis in emerging markets. In addition, country debt in emerging markets rose from 150% of GDP in 2009 to 195% in 2015, while corporate debt surged from less than 50% in 2009 to 75% of GDP in 2015. Lower economic growth in emerging markets, weak commodity prices, the stronger dollar and the expected increase of the interest rates in the US dam the flood of cheap capital. Debt cycles may end in crisis and recession: the challenge is to identify how much pain still lies ahead of us. To try and answer this we have to identify the Key Predictive Indicators such as pressure on the profitability of multinationals, and the decrease in cash flow of exporting companies.

You can get these kinds of insights not from data-information gathering on markets, nor from analysis of industry sectors or competitive intelligence, but from foresight gained from strategic intelligence.

"We have to realize that sustainable future growth in Europe is an illusion as long as the average debt of the 19 euro countries is 92.1% of National Income, while we all agreed on a maximum of 60%"

54. **Top management doesn't understand strategic intelligence**

"Why is Strategic Intelligence the most neglected management concept? Because top management doesn't understand strategic intelligence and professionals in our organizations stick too much to the short-term operational stuff"

For decades, it has been difficult to climb the intelligence pyramid from data, information, and knowledge to intelligence towards courses of action. A second point is that most of us tend to stick to the short-term operational and tactical level, because most managers are not aware of the strategic direction of the company. Peter Drucker stated that strategy is the most difficult thing in business because it means making choices that differentiate us from the competition. A third aspect is that data and information management in most organizations is generally poor!! Why is this?

Information poverty in business society

According to research conducted by PwC among 1800 business leaders in Europe and the US, only 4% of all organizations were fully capable of deriving value from the information available to them. Almost 40% of all organizations did not have the necessary resources and skills to gain value from information. Over 40% gained hardly any competitive advantage from their information, and 25% were unable to gain any benefit from their information. This research resulted in the first Information Value Index that indicated how organizations manage their information and how they are able to get benefits from it. The average result was 50.1, which means that most organizations still have a long way to go. Other crucial issues that emerged were:

➢ 20% had no data-analysts
➢ For organizations which had data-analysts, 16% lacked essential skills and 15% lacked resources
➢ Hardly any information was transformed into insights which contributed to the operating results
➢ Organizations were unable to manage the huge flows of information

By far the majority of organizations do not know what information they have available, nor do they know how this information flows through the organization. Neither do they know when the information is most valuable or most vulnerable.

How can we solve this problem?

Since 2002 many organizations have sent their personnel to our International Master Class Strategic Intelligence, recognized in Europe as the leading training course in intelligence and how to create business insights and foresight from vast flows of data and information.

Two representatives amongst many others, stated:

➤ "This Master Class showed me why we should have been in competitive intelligence yesterday", a Dutch-listed international company
➤ "It's a privilege to attend this Master Class, highly-recommended to everybody in management", a German company with 20% annual growth

"The majority of organizations don't know what information they have available, nor do they know how this information flows through the organization and in addition they do not know when the information is most valuable or most vulnerable"

55. Predictive Indicators – China

"Let's just hope shipping isn't telling the real story of China", Bloomberg Intelligence

In our daily strategic intelligence practices, we regularly list several Key Predictive Indicators (KPIs) to see what the near future might tell us. This is not forecasting. It is, however, based on delivering perspectives going beyond the brutal facts, by creating crucial foresight and early warning. Our governments, banks, the European Commission, national forecast institutes and our uncritical media tell us that we can expect economic growth. We don't believe this! Our early warning analyses indicate the opposite.

From 2008 to 2014 China dragged the world out of a second great recession. However, China's slowdown might cause a major shock to Western economies in 2018-2020. Here are some of the relevant Key Predictive Indicators:

1. The dramatic collapse of all shipping-related metrics when it comes to seaborne trade with China: the Baltic Dry Index shows record lows
2. The Shanghai Containerized Freight Index shows a strong drop
3. The China Commodity Exports Index (aluminum, steel and oil products) showed a dramatic downturn

4. Imports are weakening because of reduced spending by local governments in China, which are the dominant players in the economy
5. The central government has withdrawn its guarantees for Local Government Financing
6. Chinese steel mills have been pressured by losses, low prices and overcapacity as demand drops to levels unseen since 2009.

One might conclude that the manufacturing boom in the world's second largest economy is under fierce pressure and will impact the rest of the world. Just compare this with Europe in the event that the German economy is stagnating. Is our view pessimistic or are we being realistic? We think both; we are after all strategic intelligence professionals bringing countervailing power senior management.

"If you don't read a newspaper every day you are uninformed. If you do, you are misinformed", Mark Twain

56. **Most managers ignore small changes**

"Small changes appear one-by-one. Most managers ignore them. Managers fail to believe they will affect them. At the end management is surprised because competitors outpaced them"

"Your challenge is to look for early signs of new customer habits (1), new production technologies (2), new lateral competition (3), new regulations (4) and new means of distribution (5)"

Do you recognize these statements? What can you do about them? Do you feel accountable? A key challenge is to improve your ability to recognize and respond to signals of incremental change.

Potential Grey Swans

In Section 55, we discussed "Key Predictive Indicators" explaining the upcoming slowdown of the Chinese economy that might shock Western economies in 2018-2020. Sometimes banks also try to do this.

Let's take the example of Saxo Bank, which listed "Ten Outrageous Predictions for 2016", which we could consider as potential Grey Swans.

However, they were wrong on most of their predictions.

1. Euro-Dollar: weakening of the dollar
2. Russian ruble: up 20% by the end of 2016
3. Silicon Valley's 'unicorns' will come back down to earth
4. The Olympics will drive Brazil's recovery
5. The new US President will be a Democrat
6. OPEC turmoil will lead to higher oil prices: $ 100/b oil
7. The price of silver will increase by 30-40%
8. El Nino will spark a surge in inflation because of droughts which negatively influence agricultural production
9. Meltdown in global corporate bonds
10. Increase in inequality in Europe: 25% of the population at risk of poverty and unemployment of over 10%

De-maturity has one thing in common: executives are surprised when it happens to their industry. Small changes appear one at the time. That is the reason why executives ignore them and why they fail to believe that the changes will affect them.

"The most important challenge for management is to improve its ability to recognize and respond to signals of incremental change before the competition does"

57. The best decisions are analysis-based

"Big Ego's at the Top and how to organize Countervailing Power"

Most management models lead unnecessary and enormous cost increases with a large chance of hugely disastrous decisions, because top managers are hardly ever corrected, according to Gary Hamel. We need decisions based on responsibility and not on company position. CEOs and boards of management show 'Sun-King' behavior with too much distance from the shop-floor, leading to wrong strategic decisions.

Management of Data versus Management of Intelligence

The undeniable power of data and information brings with it the risk of becoming overly-reliant on or even obsessed by big data. The Big Data Survey 2015 by Emerce NL shows that most data is quantitative from sources such as CRM-systems, customer databases, web statistics, email statistics and transactional data. We call this data-crunching; it deals mainly with the status quo and does not deliver future-based insight or foresight. This is a similar situation to that with information, which is less of a scarce resource as it becomes ubiquitous and search costs decrease. However, the scarce resource which has to managed is no longer data and information, but attention. At senior management level, attention is fragmented, people are quickly distracted, and even when the data and information are impeccable, decisions are delayed unduly or are just plain bad. Amazon's CEO Jeff Bezos says that decisions that can be made by analysis are the best: decisions based on facts! This is strategic intelligence at its core: providing perspective over and beyond the facts.

"There are decisions that can be made by analysis. These are the best kind of decisions. They are fact-based decisions!", Jeff Bezos, CEO of Amazon

58. Six risk environments in our VUCA world

"Companies operate in an increasingly complex world: business environments are more diverse, dynamic and interconnected than ever – and far less predictable", HBR J/F 2016

Many firms still follow the traditional approaches to strategy that were designed for more stable times, emphasizing analysis and planning and focused on maximizing short-term performance rather than long-term robustness. In early 2016 Harvard Business Review published research dealing with 30,000 public US-companies over a time span of 50 years. From 2016 to 2020 public companies had a 33% chance of being delisted, because of bankruptcy, liquidation, M&A or other causes.

This 'mortality' applied regardless of size, for how many years they had existed, or sector.

The following causes were identified:

1. Failing to adapt to the growing complexity of their environment
2. Misreading the environment
3. Selecting the wrong approach to strategy
4. Failing to support a viable approach with the right behavior and capabilities

In strategic intelligence, we act in a VUCA (Volatile-Uncertain-Complex-Ambiguous) world. The HBR identified six risk environments:

1. Collapse: change from within or outside the industry renders the firm's business model obsolete
2. Contagion: shocks in one part of the economy or business ecosystem spread rapidly to other parts
3. Fat-Tail: rare but large shocks such as natural disasters, terrorism and political turmoil
4. Discontinuity: the business environment evolves abruptly in ways that are difficult to predict
5. Obsolescence: failing to adapt to changing consumer needs, competitive innovations or altered circumstances
6. Rejection: participants in the ecosystem reject the company as a partner

The dynamics and complexity of the business environment will remain strong for the foreseeable future. A paradigm shift in managerial thinking is needed: how can we win this game? And how can we extend the game? Companies must monitor the changing dynamics of their environment on a 24/7 basis and align their strategies with the threats they face. Does your organization have a company radar in place?

"There will be always someone, some company, some organization that will take over your position and your customers"

59. **Five ways to create forward-looking courses of action**

"Strategic War-Mapping forces management to get into the shoes of competition"

Companies have a tendency to compete on the basis of their core competencies rather than on the basis of those attributes that really distinguish them in the eyes of their customers. Core competencies seem to be a safe approach but are not the best route to business success. Your focus should be 'outwards-in' rather than 'inwards-out'. Firstly, one must go after the must-haves, and only secondly after the salient differentiators, so as to be able to win the game. This means changing from looking in the rear-mirror to monitoring the road ahead. Boards have to be challenged to look further out than anyone else in the company. A professional strategic intelligence team can facilitate this and help steer boards of management create the necessary forward-looking courses of action by delivering 'intelligence that cannot be ignored'. There are five ways to create those paths:

1. Analyze the external competitive landscape over and above merely looking at the traditional industry sector, by generating the outside-in insights and foresight from external sources
2. Set the strategy framework: define, outline and select the options, and determine the strategy of where-to-play and how-to-win
3. Unleash the joint knowledge, insight and foresight of key people, and execute quarterly strategic reviews
4. Anticipate the potential as well as the existential risk: the aim is to be ready for these existential risks should they occur
5. Establish a new place to set, share, and communicate and the required course of action: your company's radar room

"A company is like a person. It can't stand still. Either it moves ahead or drops back. If you are not competitive, you either become competitive or get out. It's as simple as that"

60. Strategic Intelligence in Israel

"I have attended a wide variety of training courses on Competitive Intelligence, but this Master Class Strategic Competitive Intelligence exceeded my expectations: a wide variety of intelligent and relevant tools with easily adaptable templates. I can't wait to begin using them. Thanks so much!", Iris M. Stein, Israel

The above is one of the testimonials concerning our Master Class held in Tel Aviv, Israel, in 2016 with 45 business professionals attending from a wide variety of industry sectors. It was a real challenge for us to work with these Israeli professionals in what is seen as the "cradle of the most advanced intelligence practices in the world". Our host was the Israel Export Institute. The previous day I had the opportunity to be keynote speaker on the topic "Big Ego's and How to Create Countervailing Power" hosted by FIMAT, the Israeli Competitive Intelligence Forum. Both events were successful, and highly-appreciated, and delivered new visions on strategic competitive intelligence best practices over and above all expectations. I was able to make numerous new friends in this beautiful country.

We need new talent to make it happen

We live in a VUCA world with high levels of Volatility-Uncertainty-Complexity-Ambiguity. Who is ultimately accountable to see the dynamic changes in our business environment in a timely fashion and deliver insights and foresight. Over 60% of innovation is considered to come from outside your sector of industry. According to Peter Thiel, this is not just "one-to-n", but "zero-to-one", which makes analysis of the current and future competitive arena a necessity. What do we do with risk management, big-data analysis, sales analytics, strategy, market research and strategic marketing? Can we leave these tasks to risk managers, big-data analysts, strategists, market researchers, marketers and others? Can we continue by using the current silo-approaches? Industry desperately needs people who can pull all this together, a capability which has never existed before. It requires a real mix of insight, foresight, analysis, strategy and strategic thinking with the aim of delivering the essential course of action to be taken. The talent we need for this is that possessed by strategic competitive intelligence professionals.

In our master classes on strategic competitive intelligence, we provide a wide variety of solutions. One of the most recent examples of how a Top-50 company did this, is their appointment of a "Vice-President of Strategic Intelligence & Head of Future Disasters".

"Industry desperately needs people who can pull all this together. This capability never existed before. It's a real mix of insights, foresight, analysis, strategy and strategic thinking, resulting in the essential course of action"

61. The EU is in slow-motion, but what about Silicon Wadi?

"Skyscrapers are inherently speculative and confirm the easy availability of debt. Building the tallest building is a perfect example of overconfidence and irrational exuberance. It's an early indicator of a bubble"

This statement demonstrates a potential problem. One example is that of the European Central Bank (ECB), with their new headquarters in Frankfurt, financed with even more debt in a financial world led by overconfidence and exuberance. The eurozone has been in a slow-motion crisis for some 7-8 and no one seems to be in charge: neither Draghi, Merkel, Tusk, Juncker or anyone else. The ECB doesn't stand for anything but improvisation. While the US FED prints "In God We Trust" on US dollars, the ECB might as well print "kick the can down the road" on the euro. Europeans simply react to events as they happen and hope that things don't get worse. European citizens are devoted to their holidays, their cars and their smartphones and are not prepared to make sacrifices necessary to stop destructive forces such as Putin, IS, the Iranian ayatollahs, or Erdogan, who all look primarily at achieving their own ambitions.

The military protection provided by the US has further weakened the European immune system. It seems that Europeans have chosen to live in a state of helplessness: their biggest disaster, namely Brexit, occurred on 23rd June, 2016.

What can we learn from a small start-up country?

In April 2016, I was lecturing in Tel Aviv. Israel is in a constant fight for survival and has been extremely successful with numerous start-ups. According to the March 2016 issue of Fortune Magazine, Silicon Valley has lost its 'magic' since 2000, while Israel's Silicon Wadi is enjoying huge success. Why is this? It is because of the unique combination of three drivers: young people often start their own companies after their compulsory military service (1), close connections between the business and academic worlds (2), and the well-developed local defense-industry (3). In the last 20-30 years this has resulted in there being 130 Israeli listed companies on the New York Stock Exchange, and a further 74 Israeli companies listed on Nasdaq. The 74 Nasdaq listings are more than all the listings of companies from Western Europe, Taiwan, Japan and South Korea together.

Together with my friend Dr. Avner Barnea in Israel, I have written an article about this start-up phenomenon. One reason was that in the Netherlands, the government initiated "Start-up Fest Europe", but only used presenters and business cases from Silicon Valley, relying on the usual business examples of Apple, Airbnb, Uber, Booking.com, Alphabet and others. For this reason, we stated: "The Dutch government chose the wrong direction, and should change course from West to East".

"Only executives who are flexible enough to adapt strategy to changes in competitive circumstances can effectively manage resources during competitive operations", Sun Tzu

62. Do we believe the truth when we hear it?

"Do we believe we all know the truth when we hear it, even if it's not what we want to hear, and do we feel better once we come to grips with reality?"

Do we really believe the truth when we hear it, even if it is not what we want to hear? That is strategic intelligence at its core: critical thinking, perspectives over and above facts, challenging assumptions, and determining the course of future action. On one occasion, I was presenting to one of the leading business groups in the Netherlands, and at the end, the CEO of a top-25 listed company asked us what kind of differentiating tools we use to determine the possible courses of future actions. We frequently use six for our clients: scenario planning and analysis, strategy under uncertainty, strategy as active waiting, competitive arena analysis, early warning analysis and Grey Swan analysis. He asked me to give three examples of future Grey Swans?

Note that he asked about Grey and not Black Swans: Grey Swan events are generally things we don't like to hear. Here are three examples:

1. On 31st December, 2018, the ECB will stop using € 500 notes: currently 30% of all the physical currency notes in circulation out of a total of € 1,000 billion are € 500 notes. The expected impact will be a further weakening of the euro against the dollar and the Swiss franc. Switzerland is the only country in Europe with a 1,000 Franc note, which already represents 60% of all Swiss notes in circulation. In the next couple of years € 500 notes will be exchanged for CHF 1000 notes. The ECB may not succeed in fighting financial crime, terrorism, corruption and the war on drugs, if the Swiss decide to maintain their CHF 1000 note.

2. It is expected to be tough going in Greece in the summer: Greece needs more money again, though people generally don't like to hear this. Nobody likes to hear the following: according to research by the European School of Management and Technology in Berlin, reports that 95% of the € 220 billion in Greek bailout money went to European banks, which means that only € 9.7 billion found its way into the Greek budget for the benefit of citizens. The impact is expected to be another 'hot summer' for Greece and an additional loss of faith in EU-leadership and in country leaders such as Merkel, Macron, Rutte and the other eurozone-leaders.

3. Is China back? TV entertainers and the analysts at banks tell us that China is in recovery again! But this is not the case. The Baltic Dry Index currently shows that it has plunged; this is a clear early warning signal that China is not back!

"The real truth is that much of what we were all taught is not so much how the world really works as how the world should work"

63. The Top of Intelligence is Early Warning

"The aim of Strategic Intelligence is to identify future change of significance impact, strategic crises, Grey Swans and more. Most important is delivering Early Warnings"

The core activity of our firm is to deliver strategic intelligence solutions to our clients.

You might think "So what?" We can't influence the performance of our national economies, so we have to live with it. But this totally wrong. What happens at the macro-level will influence both the mesa- and the micro-level, and so it is of direct influence on your industrial sector and your company. What then might be a wise decision? What would we do? The answer is simple: perform a strategic intelligence analysis of the competitive arena for 2019 as well as for 2020-2021 and then define your possible 'courses of future action'.

"It is easier to fool people than to convince them that they have been fooled", Mark Twain

64. Brexit

"Will a potential Brexit really become an early warning for the bureaucrats in Brussels?"

"It is clear that the EU will only move in one direction: towards more centralization, more bureaucracy, with more power shifting further away from people's hands"

The 23rd June, 2016, is a historic date in the development of the EU: it is the day on which the British voted for Brexit. Our politicians still believe that all good things in the world come as a result of their actions. However, the economic reality is that our success in trade depends far more on fundamental factors such as 'comparative advantage', and whether we design and make things that others want to buy, than on politician's bureaucratic schemes. The real choice is not economic security or economic risk as the elites at Central Banks, ECB, IMF, the Confederation of British Industry, the European Round Table of Industrialists and all the other Establishment Stooges like to tell us. They like the EU because their whole world depends on it: their lifestyle with it summit meetings, first-class flights and five-star hotels. Their flitting and floating from New York to Brussels to Beijing, serving the interests of the technocratic elite of bankers, bureaucrats and accountants, who push the same old dogmas of globalization, privatization and centralization, regardless of which government is in power in which country.

"The real choice is what kind of government will best equip us to cope with a risky fast-changing world rather than the inevitably sclerotic speed of a committee of 28 countries each with vastly different agendas, whose' leaders are unable to make the necessary decisions"

The systems and structures that the EU has designed to run the modern world have become too big, too bureaucratic and distant from the human scale. The EU has three non-elected presidents, a basic violation of the fundamentals of democracy. The elite does not want to understand that European citizens are angry and feel they have lost out due to globalization, seeing the economy moving in ways that disadvantage them and their children. They are worried about immigration and ask themselves again-and-again why their governments are so keen to help newcomers despite high unemployment rates in Greece, Spain, Italy, Netherlands, France, UK and Belgium. The elite and bureaucrats, including the entire bunch of members of the European Parliament, fail to understand why their citizens are angry. The EU has become a source of instability, sticking to an outdated script at a time of unprecedented demographic and economic change.

Imagine companies that don't listen to their customers, or know what their customers want, they would soon go out of business. But the 50,000 employees at the EU don't worry at all, because they are sure to get their salary at the end of the month. This, however, will not last: our expectation is that the EU will implode.

Why is this? For the following reasons, amongst others:

1. Nearly everyone in the EU acknowledges that the euro has been a disaster. One example is Greece
2. The euro has impoverished the countries of Southern Europe: France, Portugal, Spain, Italy and Greece
3. The high level of debt in the EU is one of the biggest problems that remains unsolved
4. Research amongst 9,500 companies across Europe in 2016 showed that 84% were not willing to invest despite extremely low interest rates
5. Meetings of G7, G20, Davos and other wasteful meetings, have not come up with any constructive proposals for reviving the global economy

6. The EU is on the cusp of a prolonged period of stagnation and instability

"Officers eat last. Yet Captain Schettino was the first to abandon the Costa Concordia. The incumbent elite is incapable of sacrifice and is too busy with their own interests to face new challenges"

65. The financial world is a mess

"The financial system is like a shared partnership where you and your partner promise to stop smoking in 2030, stop drinking in 2040, and to be loyal for half of the time in 2050. That is the current uncontrollable and unmanageable situation between governments, politicians and central bankers."

The above statement illustrates the dramatic situation in the financial markets where no one, no one at all, has any control. This is what we face daily in our strategic intelligence practices. We provide some insight as to why we cannot rely on the financial system, or on presidents, prime ministers, politicians or central bankers.

- Demand for money lags behind supply. Some of the causes are aging populations, income inequality, consumer savings and structural tax increases on the middle class
- The surplus of an increase in the money supply, and collapse in demand, has led to a savings surplus or 'savings glut'
- Savings are hit because interest rates are so extremely low, and the 'price of money' is expected to fall further
- In 2008, the bubble burst causing a worldwide deep recession. This slump was overcome when governments began to expand their debt
- The FED and ECB started with quantitative easing (QE) or 'printing money' by buying government bonds: in 2016, this reached US$ 11,000 billion worldwide, and was even more during 2017-2018
- Investment and spending by governments could solve the problems, as the current interest rates are so low
- 'Negative interest rates': how long are they going to last? This has no economic logic!
- The easing of loans keeps non-viable businesses alive, an effect called 'evergreening'. This impacts competition, and limits productivity and

thus economic growth. Banks have many of these kinds of 'bad loans' on their balance sheets
- These 'bad loans' give banks insufficient space to finance promising new initiatives
- In Italy banks have around € 360 billion of 'bad loans' on their balance sheets. Will an Italian banking crisis lead to the next financial crisis?
- Finally, if companies pay low interest during structural under-performance, we can speak about 'creative destruction'

It is obvious that the financial system can't be controlled by any one: no president, no prime minister from whatever country, no FED, no ECB, no Central Bank. Joris Luyendijk, who conducted research for 2 years in the City, expressed this well. In 2015, he wrote, regarding who is in control in the financial world the following great statement:

"Imagine you are sitting in an airplane, relaxing with a glass of wine, and when looking out of the window you see that the engine is on fire. There is no cabin crew. In the chaos you make your way to the front of the plane and open the door of the cockpit only to find that there are no pilots"

Banks try to improve their ratios by shifting risks. However, these risks remain within the financial system: the systemic risks have not been reduced since 2008, and have actually increased. On 10th July, 2016, Chief Economist Folkerts of Deutsche Bank stated that Europe must support the banks in Southern Europe with € 150 billion to prevent a new economic crisis.

66. Failures in Mergers & Acquisitions continue as 'business as usual'

"Mergers & Acquisitions is a mug's game: typically, some 70-90% of acquisitions are abysmal failures", Harvard Business Review/June 2016

This statement is the key message in a crucial publication in HBR in June 2016, about the extremely expensive mistakes in M&A, which seem to be unstoppable! This has been going on for 40-50 years! Let's look at some examples:

- Microsoft wrote off US$ 7.9 billion in 2015 after its acquisition of Nokia's handset business

- HP wrote off US$ 8.8 billion of its US$ 11.1 billion acquisition of Autonomy
- News Corporation sold MySpace for US$ 35 million after acquiring it for US$ 580 million in 2010
- Daimler-Benz wrote off US$ 35.2 billion in 2005 on the acquisition of Chrysler in 1998 of US$ 36 billion
- The merger between AOL and Time Warner for US$ 164 million was the biggest M&A failure in history

None of the acquiring companies understood their new markets, which contributed to the ultimate failure of those deals.

The article in HBR provides a simple reason why most acquisitions fail. Companies which focus on what they are going to get from an acquisition are less likely to succeed than those that focus on what they have to such a venture.

An acquirer can improve its target's competitiveness in four ways: by being a smarter provider of growth capital (1), by providing better managerial oversight (2), by transferring valuable skills (3), and by sharing valuable capabilities (4). No single one is sufficient, however all four together improve the likelihood of successful mergers and acquisitions.

Four interesting M&A's are currently in progress and/or integration. Three are expected to fail. The companies involved are:

➢ Dow Chemical and DuPont, both in the US
➢ AB InBev in Belgium, and SABMiller in the UK
➢ Bayer in Germany, and Monsanto in the US
➢ Tata Steel in the Netherlands/UK and ThyssenKrupp in Germany

Why this is this still going to happen? In our latest book "Big Boys Big Ego's and Strategic Intelligence", we explained that M&A activity is one of the fifteen key variables that determine the level of positive and destructive narcissism of CEOs.

"Narcissistic CEOs want drama, because they need attention and applause. They, therefore choose visible actions instead of slow changes to the status quo", Donald Hambrick

67. Establishing special intelligence teams to make things happen fast

"Why did US-based Citigroup establish a SWAT Team (Special Weapons and Tactics) Team?"

Citigroup established a SWAT team to take the lead from the new fintech start-ups, which are threatening the global multi-trillion-dollar banking industry. Citigroup wants to 'fintegrate' fast because they want to be ahead of the revolution, according to Fortune Magazine in July 2016.

The SWAT Team is necessary because this revolution in the banking sector cannot be managed traditional bankers. Well-funded start-ups, around 50 of them, are active in the following banking segments:

1. Investment banking: Axial, IEX, Circleup, Equidate, Angellist, Kensho – 6 start-ups
2. Retail banking: Mozido, Circle Internet Financial – 2 start-ups
3. Lending: Prosper, Sofi, Ondeck, Lendup, Avant, Funding Circle, Kabbage, Lending Club and Credit Karma – 9 start-ups
4. Treasury: Blockstream, Ripple, Digital Assets Holdings and Coinbase – 4 start-ups
5. Payments: Square, Coin, Transferwise, Stripe, Paypal and another 8-10 newcomers from the
   telecommunications sector, with spin-offs from Apple, Amazon, Samsung, Facebook and other 15-20 start-ups
6. Wealth Management: Robinhood, Wealthfront and Betterment – 3 start-ups

We all know that Apple, Facebook, Google NeXT, LinkedIn, Twitter, Android, Netflix, and WhatsApp began as 'start-ups'. Not all the start-ups in fintech will be successful, but the revolution and disruption already began several years ago, and will completely disrupt the competitive banking arena.

Citigroup used a SWAT Team to help make disruption happen. In our firm's best practices, we have established similar solutions to counteract the dynamics of future change within client organizations; we have called them: Rapid Response Team, SEALS Team, Corporate Radar Team and MI7. Our precondition to establishing these teams is that they report only to the Board of Management.

Citigroup understood perfectly that to successfully manage disruption, special strategic intelligence teams were needed.

"Intellectual courage is necessary to challenge conventional wisdom and imagine new possibilities", Rosabeth Moss Kanter

68. **Unilever's CMI and Clayton Christensen's "jobs-to-be-done"**

"The new source of competitive advantage is customer centricity: deeply understanding your customers' needs and fulfilling them better than anyone else", Unilever in Harvard Business Review 9/2016

"After decades of watching great companies fail, we have come to the conclusion that the focus on correlation and on knowing more and more about customers is taking firms in the wrong direction", Clayton Christensen in HBR 9/2016

It was interesting to read first about Unilever's Consumer and Market Insights Group (CMI), and then Christensen's comments that most companies spend too much time and money compiling data-rich models that make them masters of description but failures at prediction. Let us explain. Organizations now know more about their customers than ever before. Big-data analytics can provide an enormous variety and volume of customer information at unprecedented speed. Almost all companies have established structured, disciplined innovation processes and have brought in highly-skilled talent to run them. Structure is created to show correlations. However, correlation is not the same as causality, and most managers have grown comfortable basing decisions on correlations.

Unilever's CMI mission is "to inspire and provoke to enable transformational action". CMI implemented a global marketing information system accessible to all marketers across the organization that integrates data and presents it in a consistent format. The ultimate aim is that all users, wherever they reside in the firm, see the same information in the same way, what CMI calls "one version of the truth". CMI is a fully independent function with a direct line to the CEO.

Jobs-to-be-done was developed as a complement to Clayton Christensen's theory of disruptive innovation, which at its core was about competitive responses to innovation. However, the disruption theory does provide a solution of how to create products and services that customers want to buy. Jobs-to-be-done transforms the understanding of customer choice in a way that no amount of data ever could, because it gets at the causal drivers behind a purchase. Successful innovation helps consumers solve problems: it can be both much more predictable and profitable if you begin by identifying jobs that customers are struggling to get done.

Both Unilever's CMI and Clayton Christensen's Jobs-to-be-done are ideal solutions designed to meet future customer needs. Unilever's CMI solution is almost similar to solutions that our firm created some years ago with our Corporate Radar Room, SWAT and SEALS Teams and MI7, which, however, went far beyond the limited scope of marketing at Unilever's CMI Group.

"79% of insight functions at overperforming companies participated in strategic decision-making at all levels of the organization, compared with just 47% at underperforming companies", Insights 2020

69. Income inequality will have a huge impact on everything

"Governments across the EU are killing the middle class with income inequality which will have a huge and negative impact on the prosperity of 70 – 80% of the total EU population from 2016 – 2025"

This statement comes from McKinsey publications in July and August 2016 on 'income inequality'. This new reality means that a new generation of young people in Europe and the US risks ending up poorer than their parents. From 2005-2014 around 65-70% of the population faced flat or falling incomes. Prior to 2005, this percentage was just 2%. This means that 65-70% of the total population faced a lack of economic progress. The main causes were the aftermath of the 2008 financial crisis and the slow recovery that occurred since then. What are the implications?

1. Everyone wants their children to progress and be better off than they were. For many people, however, this will be deeply disappointing
2. There will be slower economic growth because the vast majority has less to spend
3. Rising social tensions: with people worried about free trade, globalization, technology and migration

In the years before 2005, only some 2% of the population was not advancing, and this was not a big issue for governments when compared to issues such as unemployment and economic growth. The labor markets are still not really working for the vast majority of people.

What may have worked in the past, does not work in the present: technology is replacing jobs (1), there is an increase in the number of jobs moving overseas through trade, offshoring and other factors (2), and finally there are the issues of migration and immigration (3). Over 200 million people no longer live in their home countries.

These developments are not good for the economies of countries in the EU. From 2016 to 2025, around 70-80% of the total population can expect to face flat to low rates of economic growth, high rates of unemployment, underemployment, falling wages and rising social tensions. As a result, savings will increase and spending by the middle class will stay flat.

What is the strategic impact of these developments?

The impact on the majority of companies as well as on society will be dramatic: lower investment, continuous cost-cutting, layoffs, less jobs due to robotics, underemployment, falling wages and more. In the next section, we will discuss insights as to what is happening in the US regarding the decline of the middle class from 61% in 2008, to 51% in 2016!!

"Automation and robotics will strongly increase in the next few years. As a result, wages will stay flat, although productivity will grow. According to McKinsey, this is called coupling of wages with productivity"

70. The invisible American

"We haven't seen this since the Great Depression", CEO of Gallup US on "The Invisible American"

In the fall of 2016, newspapers such as The New York Times and Financial Times published articles on the recovery of the economy. Is this really the case? It seems we cannot rely on these articles in these otherwise highly-regarded newspapers. From 2001 to 2016 the percentage of the upper-middle and middle class in the US fell from 63% to 51%. This means that some 25 million American economic lives crashed. What is missing is that these 25 million people are invisible in the widely-reported official US unemployment rate of 4.9%. Middle class jobs with average salary levels of

US$ 65,000 disappeared in our changing, disrupted and globalized world, and were replaced by full-time jobs with much lower hourly wages, equivalent to an average annual salary of US$ 30,000. The 25 million Americans remain counted as 'fully-employed' with drastically reduced pay and benefits. They fell out of the middle class and are invisible in the current statistics.

Most disastrous is the emotional toll on millions of Americans: the sudden loss of household income causing a crash of self-esteem, and dignity, leading to an atmosphere of desperation that has not been seen since the Great Depression, according to Gallup. In addition to the traditional unemployment rates, we now face a new phenomenon: underemployment.

Four serious metrics need to be turned around to prevent the loss of the middle class:

1. The percentage of the total US adult population with a full-time job has been hovering around 48% since 2010
2. From 1995 to 2015 the number of publicly-listed companies in the US fell from 7,300 to 3,700, leading to massive losses of middle-class jobs
3. New business start-ups are at historic low, however 65% of all new jobs are created by those small businesses, not by the large ones
4. From 1980 to 2010 the US consistently averaged a surplus of 120,000 more business births than deaths each year. But this has not been happening for the last 6-8 years. This is a dramatic change!

What is the strategic impact to us in Europe?

The situation in the US is not unique! The same situation has unfolded in most European countries since the beginning of the crisis in 2008. However, our governments, the EU and our politicians, continue to rely on traditional metrics including unemployment, inflation, interest rates, growth rates, and budget debt. This explains why the economic situation in most European countries is stable. Politicians do not understand that the crucial cause of stagnation in Europe is underemployment: we do not expect this situation to improve during the coming 6-8 years.

"Governments of most EU countries kill the middle class with income inequality, causing a huge impact on the prosperity of 70-80% of the total population in the EU from 2016-2025. The cause is underemployment"

71. Grey Swan Analysis

"Brexit is increasingly used by Tusk, Junker and other elites as a scapegoat for a financial crisis that has already been broiling for years and is now ready to burst into flames"

This statement has been discussed, and the big challenge in such circumstances is to identify what factors drive them. To find out, we use our Grey Swan Analysis. We have listed twelve Grey Swans which we see as, some of, the driving forces which will weaken the economic climate across Europe.

1. The US elections were between the 'Bad' and the 'Ugly'
2. The ticking time-bomb in the EU called Deutsche Bank
3. The potential banking crisis in the financial sector due to the weak positions of banks in Portugal, Spain, Italy and Greece
4. Draghi's Quantitative Easing of the ECB, which continues to print billions month-after-month
5. Interest rates across Europe of 0.1% to -/-0.5%, which are having a dramatic impact on consumer savings
6. The lack of real growth of over and above 1.5% across Europe
7. Dramatic and stable high unemployment rates across European countries
8. Potential disruptions such as FinTech, Block Chain, Robotics, and Artificial Intelligence which may all lead to numerous additional layoffs
9. The disappearing middle class leads to less consumer spending as the engine of economic growth
10. The growth of underemployment leads to growing poverty across Europe
11. The China-Europe Silk Road will disrupt container logistics
12. One of the consequences of immigration will lead to growing poverty among the European middle class

The challenge faced by management is to determine the current and future impact of the relevant Grey Swans on their business by plotting them on a scale of 'level of certainty – probability'. The impact will be huge. We strongly recommend that company management executes such a Grey Swans analysis on a quarterly basis.

"More and more people don't trust their elites. They don't trust their business leaders or their political leaders", Wolfgang Schäuble, Finance Minister of Germany

72. Deutsche Bank and more debt

"We live in a VUCA world, of Volatility-Uncertainty-Complexity-Ambiguity, which drives our strategic intelligence practices. However, no one can get a grip on the global debt which now stands at US$ 152 trillion, excluding debts in the financial sector, according to the IMF"

"In addition, no one in the world is able to identify the size of the total debt in the financial sector. To give some perspective: Deutsche Bank alone has US$ 42 trillion in derivatives on its balance sheet"

We estimate the amount of debt in the financial world to exceed the amount of global debt of US$ 152 trillion (company, consumer and government debt) by far. In business one makes strategic and business plans as result of one's scenario plans, strategic war-mapping efforts and Grey Swan analyses with the aim of getting to the future first. However, the levels of volatility and uncertainty in 2016-2018 are extremely high, and force us to try and create maximum agility in our companies. Europe will face two large Grey Swans: the first is financial, and the second political; they might, in addition, reinforce one another.

Financial crisis

The total debt of companies, consumers and governments in 2015 was some US$ 152 trillion and this represents 225% of the total world GDP. This percentage is increasing year-after-year. Compare this with Japan, which has a similar debt situation and already faces stagnation spanning some two decades. The situation of the banks in Portugal, France, Spain, Italy and Greece is still of considerable concern. In addition, we face the 'ticking time-bomb' of Deutsche Bank which is also in a very bad shape. At the end of October 2016, Moody's stated:

"Since June 2008, the market value of Deutsche Bank's assets dropped by 35% from US$ 2.3 trillion to its current level of US$ 1.5 trillion, significantly closer to its default point of US$ 1.4 trillion." Historically, when the market value of a firm's assets falls below the default point, it is highly-likely that the firm will be unable to sell assets or raise additional capital to pay its creditors. Europe will then again face the situation of banks which are 'too big to fail'. In the fall 2017, the Central Bank of Italy saved two banks with support which totaled € 20.0 billion.

The situation in Greece is still unchanged, and Italy and France will face similar problems in the event that the ECB's Mario Draghi has to stop Quantitative Easing, which will mean printing some € 80 billion in currency each month.

Political crisis

European citizens have no influence on what will happen when Europe faces a combined financial and political crisis. A crucial question will whether the euro will survive? Each of us will face high levels of volatility, uncertainty, complexity and ambiguity, in accordance with Peter Drucker's statement below:

"There are companies that make things happen, companies that watch things happen, and companies that wondered what happened"

73. The Intellectual Yet Idiot

"We have been seeing worldwide the rebellion against the inner circle of no-skin-in-the-game policymaking 'clerks' and journalists-insiders", Nassim Nicholas Taleb, November 2016

"These are the paternalistic semi-intellectual experts who tell us what to do (1), what to eat (2), how to speak (3), how to think (4), and who to vote for (5)", Nassim Nicholas Taleb, November 2016

It is fascinating to read these quotes by Nassim Nicholas Taleb, author of the bestselling "The Black Swan" and "Antifragile". Taleb is speaking about the IYI, the Intellectual Yet Idiot, a product of modernity which has been accelerating since the mid-20th century, to reach its local maximum today, along with the broad category of people without skin in the game who have been invading many walks of life. Academic-bureaucrats seem ubiquitous in our lives but are still a small minority and are rarely seen outside specialized outlets, social media and universities. This is Taleb's explanation of what happened in India, UK's Brexit, the election of the current US President and what may happen in a number of European countries as we move towards 2020. The IYI talks about 'democracy' when it fits the IYI and 'populism' when plebeians dare to vote in a way that contradicts IYI preferences.

Only 0.5% of Big Data is analyzed

In November 2016, I attended the European conference of Strategic Competitive Intelligence Professionals in Prague and had the opportunity to speak to my fellow-key-note speaker Stephanie Hughes PhD, Associate Professor at Northern Kentucky University. She presented three interesting facts: 90% of world's data was created in the last 2 years (1), 80% of the world's digital data is unstructured (2), and only 0.5% of Big Data is analyzed today (3). Back in 2011, Nassim Nicholas Taleb made some crucial observations on Big Data:

1. The more data you research, the more patterns you discover which are purely a coincidence
2. In addition, these patterns do not repeat themselves
3. People who love big data are not scientists; they may, however, have something to gain from it
4. Computer-power allowed us to create the buzzword of 'Big Data'. We always have done predictive analysis

The ICT industry, thousands of business consultancies, and the conference and seminar sector, have overwhelmed the business world with Big Data hype. In 1999-2000, we had the 'buzz of the millennium', followed by 'the buzz of cloud computing'. We now have 'the buzz of Big Data' and the next to come is 'the buzz of artificial intelligence'. Below is a pertinent quote connecting 'teenage sex' with Big Data ... So as not to miss the current hype, companies across the world have invested billions of US dollars in Big Data!

"Big Data is like teenage sex. Everyone talks about it, nobody really knows how to do it, everyone thinks everyone is doing it, so everyone claims they are doing it"

74. Geopolitical tensions and strategic intelligence

"The growing connected complexity in the world combined with growing geopolitical tensions is forcing companies to identify geopolitics which have a potential impact on their competitiveness"

"Many companies are aware of the growing risks in the external business environment, however, not that many are able to manage these risks proactively"

The world did not face many geopolitical tensions during the period from 1998 to 2008. After the fall of the Berlin Wall, we saw Pax Americana at its peak together with the Great Moderation: we experienced low inflation, low interest rates, stable economic growth, low rates of unemployment and the rise of the BRIC-countries. During this period, the number of business connections increased exponentially: as did interrelationships between companies and international markets, foreign suppliers, new production locations and global financial markets. The results were cost-efficiency, diversification and new markets, as well as growth of the interdependence of both geopolitical and macro-economic developments. This works well in periods of growing interdependence. But because of US misadventures in Iraq and Afghanistan, the financial, economic and euro debt crises, conflicts in 2017-2018 now concern geopolitical-economic events such as financial and economic sanctions, boycotts, exchange-rate manipulations, interest rates because of QE, amongst others. Many companies are aware of these developments, but only a few, however, are able to manage these proactively.

Identifying the potential risk with strategic intelligence

Companies can prepare themselves proactively for the strategic risks in their external business environment. This is strategic intelligence at its core! With strategic intelligence tools such as 'Strategy under Uncertainty', 'War-Gaming', 'Grey Swan Analysis', and 'Corporate Radar Rooms', we are able to identify relevant potential risks and uncertainties. After plotting them visually on an uncertainty and probability scale, we can analyze their impact. Companies do not operate as separate islands and remarks such as "it's not going to happen to us" are collectively naïve. Companies are now an integral part of international society. Although we are unable to influence external risks, we can, nevertheless, identify them, analyze their impact, and mitigate their potential consequences on our own organization. Again, this is strategic intelligence at its core!

Strategic intelligence goes beyond data collection, big-data analytics, and market and competitive intelligence, towards integrating all the crucial elements of significance which may have a future impact on the performance of our companies.

"Fools have a great advantage over the wise, they are always self-satisfied", Napoleon Bonaparte

75. The Strategic Five

A great strategy is "unique, specific and complete" or as Michael Porter has stated, "Strategy is about making choices differently from your rivals"

In our strategic intelligence practices, we see many misunderstandings about strategy. Firstly, many of us see strategy as 'strategy concepts' such as SWOT-analysis, Five Forces, Value-Chain Strategy, Scenario Planning, Customer Loyalty, Core Competencies, Blue Ocean Strategy and others, many of which have largely faded after enjoying a few years of attention and acclaim. Secondly, strategy concepts too often conflate goals with ideas: they try to maximize speed, increase quality, maximize net promotor score, or expand growth horizons. But these are simply generic goals that any company might adopt. Thirdly, there is a confusion between the words 'strategy' and 'strategic', meaning something which is important, which makes 'strategic' the most misused word in management today.

Great strategies always go against the grain of accepted wisdom. The basics are big ideas that provide novel solutions to specific problems unique to particular companies. Capable strategists know that great strategies are like children: you never love someone's else's as much as you love your own. This means that leaders must be their own strategists.

Strategy can never stand still because one should always seek ways to open one's eyes to new possibilities. But there are two big ifs:

1. If you do not already have a strategy to which you are truly committed, you may be particularly vulnerable to being blinded by the latest strategy fashion

2. If you do not have a strategy, begin the hard work of identifying the big idea of formulating a unique, specific and complete set of answers to the 'Strategic Five' questions below:

The Strategic Five are the critical questions your strategy should answer:

1. What business or businesses should your company be in?
2. How should you add value to your businesses?
3. Who should be the target customers for your businesses?
4. What should your value propositions be to those target customers?
5. What capabilities should differentiate your ability to add value to your businesses and deliver their value propositions?

"Great strategies are like children: You never love someone else's children as much as you love your own"

76. **The Blue-Ribbon List**

"We cannot change what we are not aware of, and once we are aware, we cannot help but change"

In December 2016, Fortune Magazine published a 'Blue-Ribbon List' of some 34 companies, based on a combination of seven ratings from Fortune 500, Global 500, Best Companies to Work For, Change the World List, World's Most Admired Companies, 100 Fastest-Growing Companies and Business Person of the Year.

*   The top-10 companies were: Alphabet, Gilad Sciences, Nike, Accenture, Amazon, American Express, Apple, Bank of America, Capital One, Centene
*   In positions 11-20: Cisco, Coca-Cola, CVS Health, Facebook, General Dynamics, General Electric, General Motors, Goldman Sachs, IBM and Intel
*   In positions 21-34: J&J, Mastercard, McDonalds, Microsoft, Netflix, PepsiCo, Publix Retail, Salesforce, Starbucks, United Continental, United Technologies, USAA, Walmart and Walt Disney

We know most these companies. All have a clear strategic direction with a concise set of choices that determines what they do and what they do not do. That is what makes them so successful. The list includes a combination of long-existing corporates, and new companies established since the 1980s, such as Alphabet, Amazon, Apple, Netflix, Salesforce and Starbucks. Each of them also leads in their respective competitive arenas.

"We are living in a world where we need to completely understand our environment and then look for anomalies, look for change, and focus on change"

77. The credibility and reliability of information

"Experts speak in two different ways: firstly, by evaluating and combining facts and evidence, and based on this, drawing their conclusions, and secondly by just giving their opinion"

Increasingly, 'experts' limit themselves by just giving their opinion. We saw this happening when CNN broadcast their opinion about Trump and his connections with Russia two hours before the press conference at 5 pm on Wednesday 11th January, 2017. CNN's 'breaking news' resulted in complete chaos. When this happens we always ask ourselves three questions: is this 'cherry-picking', resulting from selecting only the data which fits in a particular hypothesis? (1), is it 'selective windowing' meaning the simple creation of headlines in the media? (2), or is it a case of 'counter-knowledge' meaning incorrect information packaged as fact? (3).

In our strategic intelligence best practices, we always analyze the credibility of information and the reliability of sources on a scale of 1-6. We will explain this:

- Credibility of Information: information which is confirmed by other sources (=1), probably true (=2), possibly true (=3), doubtful (=4), improbable (=5), or, the truth cannot be judged (=6)
- Reliability of Sources: completely reliable (=1), usually reliable (=2), fairly reliable (=3), not usually reliable (=4), unreliable (=5), or, the reliability cannot be judged (=6)

The next step is to plot the results on a probability scale which varies from near certainty (8), through very likely (7), probably (6), evenly balanced (5), chance (4), unlikely (3), and very unlikely (2), to remote (1). We have been active in strategic intelligence as an independent consultancy firm since 1985, and we cannot conceive of delivering intelligence without some control of the credibility and reliability regarding the credibility of the information and reliability of the information sources that we utilize.

"It ain't what you don't know that gets you into trouble. It's what you know for sure that just ain't so", Mark Twain

78. Company mortality rates are rising

"We often hear that 80% of the big Fortune 500 companies, which were in existence before 1980, are no longer around, and that another 17% probably won't be here in five years". But what about all the other companies listed on US stock markets?

What is the scary truth about company survival? Most managers react "this is not going to happen to us". We think this is very naive!

It is interesting to analyze the research of Professor Vijay Govindarajan published in Harvard Business Review in 12/2016, which deals with some 29,700 companies listed on US stock markets. Companies listed before 1970 had a 92% chance of surviving for the next five years. However, those companies listed from 2000 to 2010 had only a 63% chance, despite the dotcom bust and the Great Recession. This shows that company mortality rates are rising! How and why can this be prevented? It turns out that companies listed after 2000 spent more than twice as much on organizational capital (personnel, patents, R&D, and IP) and only half as much on physical assets (plant and equipment) as those listed earlier. The newer companies are grounded in novel business models which give them an advantage over more traditional production companies. They are nimbler. But the bad news for these nimble companies is that their days are numbered unless they can innovate continually.

This pessimistic view is driven by a simple fact: digital companies are far more vulnerable to quick imitation. So such companies should, firstly, incorporate both technology and physical products into their business models to gain a competitive edge. And secondly, they should strive for business models that include strong network effects. Thirdly, they should increase their focus on continual innovation. Basically, this is all about competitiveness.

Do you have an idea how to prevent the demise of companies?

To get the timely insights and foresight necessary to resist the storms of discontinuous change, innovation, disruptive technologies, fierce and new competition, and new strategies, you cannot rely only on your current methodologies. You have to take an important additional step to avoid the most-asked question in business today: why didn't we see this coming? The answer is clear. Create the perfect combination of strategic intelligence – strategic thinking – leadership by establishing a SWAT Team and a Company Radar Room.

"You get the need-to-know insights & foresight by combining strategic intelligence – strategic thinking – leadership with a SWAT Team and a Company Radar Room"

79. Governments are corrupt to the bone

Following the results of the elections in the Netherlands, France and Germany in 2017, we can only agree with the famous economist Dr. Arthur Laffer, that "Governments are corrupt to the bone"

Dr. Arthur Laffer is known for his famous 'Laffer Curve'. He was a member of President Reagan's Economic Policy Board and an advisor to Prime Minister Margaret Thatcher. In January 2017, he visited the Netherlands and made statements to the effect that "governments are corrupt to the bone", and the EU is "a state-run organization where the people don't have a vote". Arthur Laffer is correct, but what is of crucial concern is the non-critical attitude of the media and journalists. What we are lacking are investigative journalists who criticize our government and politicians. We list the following seven critical issues:

1. Cherry-picking: selecting only that data and information which fits your hypothesis
2. Selective windowing: limiting yourself to the headlines in newspapers
3. Counter-knowledge: incorrect information is packaged as fact
4. Statistics are not facts, but interpretations, dependent on: the way the numbers are collected (by people!), how they are interpreted, and how they are visualized
5. Credibility of information: is this confirmed by other sources?
6. Reliability of sources: ranging from completely reliable to cannot be judged
7. Number of sources: never rely on one single source

Knowledge is a bunch of facts. Possessing much knowledge is not the same as being intelligent, however, we can adopt Leonardo da Vinci's comment, namely "learn how to see and realize that everything connects to everything else"

"The problem with people is not that they don't know, but that they know so much that is not true", Josh Willings

80. Why so many people get it wrong in strategic planning

"Strategic planning is really a competition for resources. All those vying for their share of the capital spending budget put forward 'hockey-stick plans', and you would be mad not to play along"

"One wonders why so many smart well-intentioned people can get it so wrong time after time in strategic planning"

The statements above come from McKinsey in March 2017 writing about strategic planning. How come? People are overly confident and optimistic, and informed people are even more confident (1). No one was ever promoted for putting forward a plan whose growth forecasts didn't sail upwards? (2). Executives constantly tell themselves that they need an ambitious vision to inspire great performance (3). But when the strategy outcome is not realized after the first year, attribution bias usually kicks in: one simply blames the circumstances or others, but never oneself. This implies that management is in most cases just looking at year one. Strategic planning becomes merely the set-up for the real conversation: limited to budgets and KPIs for next year! It seems that nothing has changed in the past 20 to 25 years. McKinsey untangled two opposing errors that people make: the first is of being excessively bold in making forecasts, and the second is of being excessively timid in making choices.

The fallacy that underlies most strategies is expressed by: "I will get better results next year by trying to do roughly the same thing as last year but just a little bit better". This is nothing more than hope and hot air!

There are four ways to improve this:

1. Reconcile previous plans with what actually happened, and figure out why your team failed to reach the targets it set
2. Calibrate your results to the 'outside view': this is the core of Strategic Competitive Intelligence
3. Build a momentum case: throw out the baseline forecast and start by projecting what will happen if management takes their hands off the wheel
4. Focus on moves, not promises: avoid confusing goals with strategies, which is one of the biggest mistakes in the boardroom

Many strategic-planning activities are far more focused on setting goals than on crafting choices and the necessary moves to meet those goals.

"Most strategic-planning efforts rely on the 'inside view', which is a breeding ground for all sorts of biases that subconsciously give more weight to facts that back your view than the inconvenient ones that don't"

81. All too often we tell management what they want to hear

The Number One challenge facing CEOs has two forms – "People telling you what they think you want to hear, and people being fearful of telling you things they believe you don't want to hear", Walt Bettinger, CEO of Charles Schwab

"Many times, the question is harder than the answer. If you can phrase the question properly, then the answer is the easy part", Elon Musk, CEO of Tesla

An important issue in HBR in March/April 2017, dealt with information that challenges your assumptions and allows you to perceive a looming threat or opportunity. When a dramatic shift is on the horizon, the first indications may usually appear in ambiguous events on the fringes of the market. A key problem is getting information that senior management have not demanded because they do not know how to ask for it. Often, this may be a development brewing that may ultimately redraw the lines of competition for the future. One way to describe the unanticipated risks became famous in 2002 as 'unknown unknowns', thanks to Donald Rumsfeld, the former US Secretary of Defense. He spoke about:

1. Known knowns - what we know we know
2. Known unknowns - what we know we do not know
3. Unknown unknowns - what we don't know we don't know

The worst casualties can happen when a company is blind-sighted by innovation and new players, which management never even imagined.

Below are five examples, three from HBR and two from our own experience, of ways to ensuring that executives do not withhold information from Senior Management:

1. CEO Walt Bettinger of Charles Schwab requires "brutally honest reports" twice per month
2. CEO Marc Benioff of Salesforce regularly goes on global "listening tours" looking for weak strategic signals
3. CEO Rod Drury of Xero hosts conversations that people across the company participate in and also shares the company's strategy and market intelligence with these people
4. At Royal Dutch Shell, we co-created the Seven Guidelines of Strategic Intelligence: one of the seven is "tell management the brutal truth"
5. At Delhaize Belgium, we co-created an early-warning structure as part of a daily practice in the newly-established 'Company Radar Room'

The core of our strategic intelligence best practices is to generate the early warnings signals for future action and deliver courses of intelligence action that cannot be ignored.

"The difference between successful and unsuccessful executives is not the quality of their decision-making. The difference is that successful executives are faster to recognize bad decisions and adjust, while failing executives often dig in and try to convince people that they were right", Walt Bettinger, CEO of Charles Schwab

82. Exogenous factors drive growth in Europe

"A winning mood in Europe doesn't guarantee that the structural recovery of the European economy will last during the next couple of years. Let's look at this"

Economic indicators have improved since the summer of 2016, resulting in an accelerating positive level of economic performance in Europe and the other OECD-countries. Entrepreneurs and consumers are getting back into a good mood. The professionals in government, banks and other institutes did not see this coming. In our strategic intelligence best practices, we use the 'Strategy as Active Waiting' management tool to identify early indicators of change and create possible courses of action.

Below, we identify positive indicators which drive the winning mood, as well as some potentially negative ones which might disturb this scenario.

Seven exogenous factors have driven economic recovery in Europe since the summer of 2016:

1. Governmental policies in China have improved economic growth. One indicator is Chinese imports
2. Growth of regional exports and thus production. Exports have increased in Japan (+11%), South Korea (+27%) and Taiwan (29%)
3. Divestments in the oil & gas sector stopped when the price of oil price reached US$ 30.00 in mid-June 2016. The relevant indicator is the rising oil price
4. Stock supplies decreased and stopped by mid-June 2016. Production levels are again increasing
5. Worldwide growth of investment in IT. This means more activity and future productivity growth. The relevant indicator is the SOX-index, the index of stock prices of electronics companies
6. Stopping cost-cutting by the majority of governments. The relevant indicator here is the consumer trust index
7. Recovery of assets for consumers, companies and banks, has almost been completed. Here the relevant indicator is consumer spending

There are four exogenous factors which drive negative economic recovery and which might apply in the short-term:

1. Elections in France, Germany in 2017 and in Italy in 2018
2. Negative influences resulting from the Brexit-process
3. Down turn leading to a renewed debt crisis in Greece and may be Italy
4. Increase of inflation and monetary policy in the US

It is amazing that the acceleration in the recovery of the global economy was hardly foreseen. If management can identify the right applicable exogenous factors and monitor these continuously using its company radar, this can enable them to foresee changes in the economic climate in a timely fashion before anyone else.

"It's compellingly seductive to try to predict the future as through it were a quantifiable extrapolation of the past"

83. Critical questions and challenging assumptions are core in strategic intelligence

"If we don't ask management the critical questions, if we don't challenge their assumptions and if we think they know, we are collectively naive". This does not fit within Strategic Intelligence

It has been instructive to see the following three things happening which people tend to accept far too easily: how effective are Boards of Directors, and what of their responsibility and accountability in controlling and monitoring their Boards of Management? It seems they are not effective at all, most have no idea of what is really going on, and what new challenges that are facing. Here are three examples:

1. German Automotive Industry:
   German car manufacturers Mercedes Benz, BMW, and VW/Audi are lagging behind key market developments. The BMW i3 has a range of 160km versus a Tesla with a range of 500km. Audi expects to have an electric car in 2018, Porsche-VW in 2019 and BMW in 2020. The German car industry underestimated the mega-trend of electric cars. Tesla was founded in 2003 in Silicon Valley, and launched their first electric car in 2008, followed by the Tesla S in 2012. It is incredible that

the Germans have lagged behind for so many years. In 2016, Daimler-Benz's CEO Dieter Zetsche stated: "not one producer has earned one euro with electric cars". Given this, it is strange to see that in March 2017, Daimler-Benz decided to invest € 10 billion in the development of electric Mercedes Benz cars. In addition, the French Automotive Group PSA acquired German Opel Cars because of the advanced technology of the Opel Ampera with its range of 520km.

2. Potential Acquisitions of two Dutch multinationals:
   In the Netherlands we experienced two potential hostile takeovers of two multinational companies: AkzoNobel by US company PPG and Unilever by US company KraftHeinz Food Group. The Boards of Directors of both AkzoNobel and Unilever explained the American interest because of the low cost of financing acquisitions, the low exchange-rate of the euro versus the dollar, and because European companies are rather 'cheap' compared to US companies. However, the real reason why they are acquisition targets is a combination of a lack of focus and aggressiveness, weak operational competitive strategies, poor strategies and weak top management.

3. Italy's Central Bank President Ignazio Visco:
   With the approval of Jean-Claude Junker, Italy's Central Banker has stowed away € 350 billion by means of 'creative' bookkeeping. How was this achieved? There are some € 350 billion of 'bad loans' on the balance sheets of Italian banks. Arrangements have been made for about 50% of these, which leaves some € 175 billion. The majority of this € 175 seems not to be 'hopeless', which leaves just € 87.5 billion. Of this € 87.5 billion only € 20 billion actually 'sits' on the balance sheets of 'problem banks'. The book value of this € 20 billion is just 40%, or € 8 billion. And this leaves just € 12 billion, an amount which fits neatly in the budgeted Relief Fund of the Italian Central Bank of € 20 billion. A key question is therefore: "Who is cheating who?"

Strategic Intelligence is the management of insight, foresight, analyses, strategy and strategic thinking, with deliverables such as scenario planning, war-mapping, Grey Swan analysis, strategy under uncertainty, and strategy as active waiting, resulting in the delivery of actionable courses of future action.

"There are not that many organizations that have the strategic intelligence professionals in place to tell top management the brutal truth"

84. President Macron and the EU

"What is the impact of newly elected President Macron on France and on the EU? We are increasingly ruled by an intellectual, political, economic, and cultural elite, that does not bear the consequences of the decisions it makes on our behalf", Nassim Nicholas Taleb

The French writer Charles Maurras (1868-1952) believed there were 'Two Frances': one was the 'real' France, and the other the 'legal' France. The 'real country' is the rural France of church clocks, traditions and native people fused with their ancestral soil, versus the 'legal country' which is the secular republic run by functionaries conspiring for foreign interests. When sufficient people in the country come to understand the failure of 'legal' France, they will want the 'real' France back. That will be true in countries all over Europe. As Marine Le Pen stated: "France will be led by a woman, either me or Mrs. Merkel"

Will Macron succeed in reforming the EU?
Macron wants to reform the EU. Firstly, he wants the EU to get its own budget, financed partly from VAT-revenues, from social security funds, and from the pension funds of all of the 27-member countries of the EU. Secondly, he wants to appoint an EU Minister of Finance. Thirdly, he wants to have Eurobonds. In other words, he wants to reform the EU with more integration, in contradiction to what European citizens really want.

So, will he succeed in reforming France?
The French Government is controlled by an elite consisting of politicians, bureaucrats and the military, all centralized in Paris. They all benefit from numerous privileges, which they clearly do not wish to relinquish. The elite still sticks to the illusion that it is Paris that determines what should happen in France as well as in the rest of the world. It still refuses to understand what is going on in and around France: globalization, six million Muslims in France, structurally high unemployment rates, the euro and the EU. The suburbs in French cities are 'no-go areas' beyond the control of the authorities. The unions block every reform. The country has essentially been in a state of emergency since the late 1980s.

What is the impact on the EU?
The elite in Paris who behave as 'kingdoms with financial privileges' are still unable to face reality. Former Presidents Mitterrand, Chirac, Sarkozy and Hollande all tried to reform the country, and all failed. These are the 'hard facts', and we foresee that the new President Macron will also be not unable to realize the necessary reforms. This implies that Macron, together with Angela Merkel, will move for more integration within the EU: shifting more sovereignty to Brussels means that Brussels will get even more power.

"The 'Stiglitz Syndrome' is the process whereby public intellectuals suffer no financial or career consequences for being spectacularly wrong in their predictions", Nassim Nicholas Taleb

"If I had an hour to solve a problem, I would spend the first 55 minutes determining the right question to ask. For once I knew the right question, I could solve the problem in less than 5 minutes", Albert Einstein

85. Crucial questions in business today

In Strategic Intelligence the most crucial and most frequently used word is 'why'

Asking the right questions is the biggest issue to challenge top management. Examples of crucial questions include: how long will our sources of competitive advantage survive in the face of technological shifts? How will changing customer and societal expectations affect our business models? What does it mean to be an international company when the benefits of international integration are under intense scrutiny?

Management today needs to rethink how and where they compete, and they have to identify both current and future trends which impact company performance. You must see this positively, because "the trend is your friend".

Four questions can help you frame the problems before solving them:

1. What are the megatrends that will reshape your business environment? The challenge is to identify what forces drive these megatrends
2. How will these megatrends disrupt your sector of industry and your businesses? The challenge is to tear down both these megatrends and driving forces so that you can act by reaction, or better still, by anticipation
3. What are the most uncertain issues which have the highest impact on the company? The challenge here is to create answers aligned with scenario-planning techniques
4. What are the implications of the potential scenarios? The final challenge is to formulate the applicable courses of future action

In framing these problems, we use a combination of Scenario Planning (1), Trend Impact Analysis (2), and Pre-Mortem Analysis (3), from our strategic intelligence solutions toolbox. This combination of applicable analysis tools helps you increase the likelihood of making better strategic choices and decisions by 30-50%.

"Strategy is like trying to ride a bicycle while you are inventing it", Igor Ansoff

86. Are multinationals at the end of their Company Life-Cycle?

Question: "Why have three Dutch multinationals - PostNL, Unilever and AkzoNobel - been targets for hostile takeovers?"

Answer: "Because those companies, as well as many other multinationals, are at the end of their Company Life-Cycle", Professor Dr. Jaap Koelewijn, Nyenrode University

The potential hostile takeovers of Unilever and AkzoNobel were a wake-up call for their respective boards of management and boards of directors, providing a reason for both companies to act, however, both moved in the wrong direction, by selling-off parts of their companies, and of course via cost-cutting. Two easily-implemented actions which helped improve shareholder value. The Big Egos at the top were no doubt very proud of themselves to have made a decision. Together with my co-author, Dr. Antoinette Rijsenbilt, we described those too Big Egos in numerous cases in our 2015 book "Big Boys Big Egos and Strategic Intelligence".

Wrong actions

The actions of selling-off parts of the company, cost-cutting and laying-off people are the relatively easy things to do, at least in the short-term. In the longer term, management ongoing focus must be on revenues, unmet customer needs, non-customers, effectiveness and innovation, with the aim of becoming more competitive. Things might get even worse if some of the 'old boys', like AkzoNobel's former CEO, Hans Wijers, succeed in convincing Dutch politicians to adopt new protective governance measures against hostile takeovers. This would make the boards of those companies even more lazy, and these companies would look like 'lame ducks'. In June 2017, Professor Jaap Koelewijn of Nyenrode University stated that companies like PostNL, Unilever, AkzoNobel are in the last phase of their company life-cycle, because these companies are inefficient, ineffective, not innovative, and unable to become leaders in their competitive arenas. New potential targets of hostile takeovers are AholdDelhaize US, Dutch Royal Philips and Swiss Nestle. Goldman Sachs stated that divestment, namely selling-off parts of the company, made hostile takeovers even easier.

Overage executives

Peter Drucker, quoted in 1986, was very clear about overage executives. "The basic rule, and one that should be clearly established, is that people who are no longer in their sixties should ease out of positions with major responsibilities. It is a sensible rule for everyone, and not only executives, to stay away from decisions if one won't be around to help bail out the company when those decisions cause trouble a few years down the road, as most of them do."

"The aim of Strategic Intelligence is to prevent senior management from looking like fools a few years down the road, because they took the wrong decisions"

87. Defense and offense data, and crucial other dimensions

"Less than 1% of unstructured data is analyzed, 70% of employees have access to data they don't need, and 80% of analysts' time is spent in simply discovering and preparing data", HBR M/J 2017

"The more data you research, the more patterns you discover which are purely a coincidence. In addition, these patterns will not repeat themselves. Computer-power has enabled us to create the buzz word of Big Data", Nassim Nicholas Taleb author of the Black Swan and Antifragile

The quotes are dramatic. The IT-world would like us to believe that Big Data is a success, with the emergence of all kind of data-management functions, data scientists, chief data officers and others. You might ask yourself how effective all of this is in the absence of a coherent strategy for organizing, governing, analyzing and deploying an organization's information needs. The quote by the renowned author of the famous book "The Black Swan" is also clear in this regard. In the 2017 May/June issue of Harvard Business Review, Thomas Davenport draws a distinction between data defense and offense, and other crucial dimensions.

Defense data means minimizing downside risks and includes ensuring compliance with regulations, using analytics to detect and limit fraud, and building systems to prevent theft. Data offense supports business objectives such as increasing revenues, profitability and customer satisfaction. Another dimension is the difference between a Single Source of Truth that might work at the data level, and Multiple Versions of the Truth, which supports the management of information. Finally, there is the difference between data architecture and information architecture. 'Data architecture' describes how data is collected, stored, transformed, distributed and consumed, while 'information architecture' governs the processes and rules that covert data into useful information. According to Peter Drucker "information is data endowed with relevance and purpose".

"If you torture data long enough, it will confess"

Impact on strategic intelligence

If the vast majority of companies struggle to enrich their data, you might ask yourself how is it that they are able to transform information and knowledge into intelligence. It is alarming that only a limited number of companies have state-of-art strategic intelligence in place, meaning those organizations have made the transformation from data, information and knowledge to full-scale intelligence. Those organizations have strategic intelligence-driven strategies in place, delivering real-time insight and foresight as to the crucial potential changes and dynamics that the company will face. The result is those courses of actionable intelligence which top management cannot ignore. The Company Radar Room is the place to be, as it allows management to overcome facing the most-asked question in business today, namely: "Why didn't we see this coming?"

"Do you think you can still be in business tomorrow, if you continue to use yesterday's management methodologies and techniques?"

88. Six reasons why managers have it often so wrong

"In making of strategic decisions, optimism not only generates unrealistic forecasts but also leads future challenges to be underestimated because of human biases"

Biases are predispositions of a psychological, sociological and physiological nature that can influence decision-making. We may acknowledge their existence, and yet we often believe that we are not prone to bias; in itself this is a type of bias – 'overconfidence'. Below are six reasons why so many people get this so wrong so often:

1. We are overly confident and optimistic by gathering data to support our hypotheses
2. No one ever got promoted for forecasts that do not purport to show an increase?
3. We create ambitious visions to inspire great performance
4. The phenomenon of 'attribution bias', whereby missed targets are blamed on the most convenient cause available
5. Strategic reviews are lacking: in too many cases, the strategy process becomes simply the way towards next year's budget and KPIs

6. We fool ourselves trying to achieve better results next year by trying to do roughly the same thing as we did this year, however just a little better

Every year after the summer, organizations often activate again their strategic business plans for the following year, in what therefore becomes a calendar-driven activity. Another way to do this is to go to a pleasant and remote area to discuss next year's strategic issues with SWOT-analysis as a centralized tool. Does 'strategic' mean 'important' in this case? Yes. You can see this as an 'inside view' and a breeding ground for all sorts of biases that consistently give more weight to facts that back the prevailing management view rather than the inconvenient ones that do not! The only powerful effort way to overcome this is to get into the world of strategic intelligence.

In 'debiasing', we recommend using the most-effective tools, those of structured analysis. In our International Master Class Strategic Intelligence, we teach managers how to deal with strategic planning and strategic intelligence by presenting our toolbox with the most crucial and most-effective structured analysis tools. Here we list some of these: SWOTI 2.0, Strategy under Uncertainty, Strategic War-Mapping, Grey Swan Analysis, Where-To-Play and How-To-Win, Identifying the SSS (Strategic Sweet Spot), Pre-mortem Analysis and others.

"An inside view is a breeding ground for all sorts of biases that consistently give more weight to facts that back our view than the inconvenient ones that don't"

89. Test your company's strategy

"After the summer holidays, the majority of management teams make their business plans which consist mainly of next year's budget and related KPIs, using SWOT-analysis and extrapolation, and they do this as a team-effort, often in a nice, remote area"

Most of us recognize this 'annually recurring ritual' in the company planning cycle which in most cases is based on an inside view. It becomes a breeding ground for all sorts of biases that subconsciously give more weight to facts that back management's view than inconvenient ones that don't. Being inwardly-focused and not anticipating competitors' moves is remarkably superficial and is another breeding ground for competitive surprises. To overcome this, management is forced to think 'strategically' and needs evidence-based strategic intelligence.

Four drivers that affect your strategy

What are the main trends that will reshape the business environment? (1), how will these trends disrupt your industry and your business? (2), which trends have the highest impact, and what are the most uncertain issues that these disruptions might bring; what possible future scenarios do they suggest? (3), and what are the implications of these scenarios and what will your company's future courses of action be as a result? (4). An inside view can never give you the answers, only strategic intelligence efforts are able to provide the inconvenient truths of what is really going to happen in your competitive arena.

We challenge you to test your company's strategy by answering the following ten questions listed below (adapted from McKinsey).

Test your company's strategy

1. Will your strategy beat the markets?
2. Is your strategy based on authentic sources of competitive advantage?
3. Is your strategy clear as to where-to-compete and how-to-win?
4. Does your strategy drive you ahead of trends?
5. Is your strategy based on privileged insights and foresight?
6. Does your strategy embrace uncertainty?
7. Does your strategy balance commitment and flexibility?
8. Is your strategy affected by biases?
9. Do you have Is the necessary conviction to act on your strategy?
10. Have you transformed your strategy into a 'course of action'?

"New strategic competitive insights and foresight are one of the differentiating drivers to create sustainable competitive advantage. Strategic Intelligence gives you these evidence-based facts"

90. Jeff Immelt's lessons on leadership

"One weekend a month a GE officer and her/his spouse have dinner with me and my wife at our home. The next morning, I spend 4 hours talking with him or her. This is my way to hear perspectives I might not get otherwise", Jeff Immelt, CEO of GE from 2001 to 2017

"Intelligence is not found on the internet or in databases; it is, however, created by people delivering perspectives over and above facts"

It is interesting to see how Jeff Immelt created parts of his strategic intelligence picture. After Jack Welch's period of leadership (from 1980 to 2001), Jeff Immelt transformed the 125-year-old GE into a start-up, a digital industrial company. "We compete in today's world to solve tomorrow's challenges", he said, quoted in HBR September/October 2017.

After Brexit, Jeff Immelt listed seven lessons on leadership:

1. We are witnessing the failure of bureaucracies in large institutions
2. Unrest is caused by a lack of leadership
3. People become afraid when there is no vision for growth
4. People become discouraged when their leaders do not want to compete for the future
5. People become victims when leadership fails
6. The future will be created by leaders who are willing to drive change
7. Change requires simpler organizations, new business models and more decentralization

"We can either dwell on politics or move forward with solutions", Jeff Immelt, CEO of GE, Fortune Magazine, August 2016

91. Black Swans, Grey Swans and Gray Rhinos

"If only 0.5 percent of all companies are able to get insights from Big-Data Analytics, can you imagine how many managers get insights from Strategic Intelligence? It's even less than 0.5 percent and is like driving using only the rearview mirror of a car."

"If governments, special agencies, and the military all invest billions in intelligence year-after-year, why is it that managers neglect strategic intelligence in their companies? The simple answer is because they all underestimate the phenomenon of 'The Gray Rhino'"

Every manager in every company business function is part of a high-impact VUCA world: Volatility – Uncertainty – Complexity – Ambiguity. In this VUCA world, Nassim Nicholas Taleb published his famous book "The Black Swan" in 2007. Based on Taleb's Black Swans, we have been using the phenomenon of Grey Swans with our unique Grey Swan Analysis. In the spring of 2016, Michele Wucker came out with her book "The Gray Rhino", on the basis of which we added 'Gray Rhino Analysis' to our strategic intelligence practices.

What is a Gray Rhino?

A Gray Rhino is a highly-probable, high-impact threat, which we ought to see coming, but which, however, we either do not see, or see but willfully choose to ignore. We consistently fail to recognize the obvious and fail to prevent highly-probable high-impact threats. The problem is not one of weak signals, but rather of weak responses to signals. In our companies, we are not good at recognizing threats or responding to these threats. Rhinos on the distant horizon begin as distant threats, and Gray Rhinos have the potential to come together to form herds. In the zoological world a herd of rhinoceroses is called a "crash".

"So, the question is not if but when a Gray Rhino will happen"

92. The phenomenon of hub firms

"The winner takes ALL – Google, Amazon, Apple, Facebook, Microsoft, Baidu, Tencent and Alibaba. These are called them 'hub firms' and they are expected to shape our collective future"

"The chance of a new Google is small, however the chance that Google takes over your customers is huge", Peter Hinssen in "The Day after Tomorrow", September 2017

Traditional companies spend much of their time monitoring start-ups. Likewise, the financial world does this by monitoring the fintech sector. Should we fear those start-ups or should we fear others? In his new book, "The Day after Tomorrow", Peter Hinssen tells us that we should fear potential new competitors who will take over interactions with customers. The following eight companies: Google, Amazon, Apple, Facebook, Microsoft, Baidu, Tencent and Alibaba, are the new 'hub firms' that will shape our collective future. This is because:

1. They dominate individual markets
2. They create and control essential connections in the networks that pervade our economies
3. They form and control crucial competitive bottlenecks
4. They are able to extract disproportionate value
5. They tip the global competitive balance

In an average company, 99% of the employees are busy with 'today' or with 'yesterday's sh*t' and they probably think that change will not happen that fast. But what will happen in the next 10-12 years with an aging population, retirement, increases in healthcare costs and disruption of labor markets? One can imagine a few unexpected events that might occur that could lead to an unemployment rate of 20% across Europe? Our social-economic system would implode. In China and Singapore, they know exactly what is going on with the digital revolution in mobility, in education and in healthcare. The new 'hub firms' know exactly where we are going.

For many companies this is the ultimate challenge. How can they deal with this? Strategic intelligence is the perfect way to give you the answers by monitoring those eight 'hub firms'. By doing this you can gain new insights, foresight, and early warning, all of which lead to new courses of action and improved decision-making. However, management might neglect this and treat this it as a Gray Rhino, as described in the previous section.

"I don't want to listen to politicians in Europe anymore. They don't have the slightest idea what is going to happen, however in China and Singapore they do", Peter Hinssen in "The Day after Tomorrow", September 2017

93. Managing the present versus managing the future

"There is an increased pressure by hedge funds on multinationals such as AkzoNobel, Unilever, Nestle, P&G, PostNL, KPN NL and some others. They promised to outperform in 2017, but in practice, however, they strongly underperformed"

"Those companies, as well as many other multinationals might be at the end of their Company Life-Cycle", Professor Dr. Jaap Koelewijn of Nyenrode University, July 2017

Professor Jaap Koelewijn's quote is telling, pointing out that a number of multinationals may be reaching the end of their company life-cycle. The financial press reports that an increasing number of hedge funds put heavy pressure on those boards of management to divest and/or to split up their companies to meet shareholder value. Management's answer throughout 2017 has typically been to make 'unrealistic' promises that they will somehow succeed in meeting shareholder expectations. In addition, they took the easy and relatively straightforward way forward of cost-cutting and increasing consumer prices.

What then is the real problem?

If those companies are not able to outperform the market, then something must be terribly wrong! Competition from regional, smaller, decisive, and entrepreneurial-driven companies is increasing, with alternative products/brands being offered which are perceived by consumers as preferable. We recognized some years ago that product managers, brand managers, marketing managers, and 'insight managers of all sorts', focus too much on customer experiences, consumer research, net promoter scores, and most recently on big data and big-data analytics. Peter Drucker, one of the most influential management consultants since WWII, always stated that companies have to execute two different strategies: the first is to defend the existing business with existing customers, but the second is to develop entrepreneurial strategies to meet unmet customer needs and to meet non-customers. After all, the number of non-customers far exceeds the number of customers!

What is the solution?

The solution lies in the difference between 'managing the present' and 'managing the future'. It derives from the difference between 'the management of comfort zones and preservation' and 'the management of uncertainty, risk and creation'. To explain this in more detail:

1. Managing the present involves: management of KPIs, unambiguous, objective data regarding linear changes affecting current customers, current and known technologies, resulting in linear innovations contributing to the reduction of risk, the elimination of ambiguity and deviation, and efficiency
2. Managing the future involves: management of weak signals and early warnings, Grey Swans, Gray Rhinos regarding non-linear changes affecting non-customers, non-traditional competitors, and new and emerging technologies resulting in non-linear innovation. This requires challenging assumptions, building new competencies, embracing risk-taking, learning, adaption and flexibility.

The aim of our core business, strategic intelligence, is to timely identify the weak signals and early warnings concerning customer and technological discontinuities, non-traditional competitors, new distribution channels, and regulatory changes, all in a timely fashion. Strategic intelligence provides the answers to almost every problem of crucial concern to senior management. However, as has long been quoted: "if generals cannot manage without good intelligence, why do CEOs think they can".

"A clear strategic direction is a concise set of choices that determines what we do and don't do"

94. The five drivers of competitive readiness

"The essence of formulating a Competitive Strategy is to relate your company to its environment", Michael Porter

"When you have created your Competitive Strategy, the essence is making strategic choices different from your rivals", Michael Porter

These are Important quotes from Michael Porter, dating from some years ago. However, the essence of strategy has not changed and will not change during the coming decade! It represents the common understanding regarding the ever-changing competitive environment, and what the company's response is to that. It represents your promise to deliver value to your customers, both now and in the future, in a way that no other company can do, in a world of VUCA. The results of competitive strategy are the financial plan, the budget and forecast. The financial plan deals with the company's expected financial performance for future periods. The budget is the financial plan for the upcoming year, and the forecast simply reflects the actual performance in the year-to-date plus the expected performance for the rest of the year.

Five drivers which can improve competitive readiness

In our strategy and strategic intelligence practice we recommend the following five drivers of competitive readiness:

1. Understand your rivals' economics – think about the key driving forces
2. Look forward, not backward – future potential competitive reactions are usually widely ignored
3. Put yourself in the mindset of the competition – execute 'strategic war-mapping'
4. Synthesize events into threats and opportunities – who has a sixth sense for Gray Rhinos?
5. Act more boldly – "know your enemies and know yourself and you will never be in danger"

Within the scope of our intelligence efforts we always show customers our "Intelligence Continuum". This consists of four levels: Competitor Data Collection (1), Industry & Competitor Analysis (2), Competitive Intelligence (3), and Strategic Intelligence (4). For the insight and foresight regarding the listed five drivers to improve competitive readiness, which are listed above, only strategic intelligence can give you the crucial insights you need: the topics of strategic significance, strategic crisis, Black Swans/Grey Swans/Gray Rhinos, current decisions on scenarios, the blind spots from technology play-mapping and more.

"In October 2017, Air Berlin Germany ran into bankruptcy because of 'the Management of Overconfidence' and Monarch Airlines UK because of 'the Management of Overestimation'"

95. Inward-looking versus outward-looking mechanisms

"Why are big companies blind to seeing new opportunities (1)? Why are big companies eager to buy start-ups and why do they succeed in killing these start-ups in record time (2)? Why are big companies unable to make the right steps without outside support (3)? Why do big companies behave like 'lame ducks' facing disruption, new business models, and new competitors, and why are they unable to react rapidly? (4)", Peter Hinssen, The Day after Tomorrow, 2017

"At IBM Europe, strategic competitive intelligence is aligned with every company function across the organization."

The above four questions are the guiding principles in Peter Hinssen's book "The Day after Tomorrow". During the past five decades we have seen many similar publications. In essence, not much has changed within our companies, which are still guided by inward-looking control-mechanisms. This remains a key problem!

What we are missing are the outward-looking opportunity-mechanisms. Below, we explain the difference.

- Inward-looking control-mechanisms include: Management Information Systems, Key performance Management, Control by KPIs, BSCs (balanced scorecards), BI-dashboards, Risk Management, Big Data analytics, Internal Audit Committees, Accountants, Boards of Directors or the Old Boys Network (friends with themselves). Who is ultimately accountable? Let's be honest. No one is!
- Outward-looking opportunity-mechanisms include: Strategy under Uncertainty, Strategy as Active Waiting, Where-to-Play/How-to-Win, Strategic War-Mapping, Grey Swan Analysis, Gray Rhino Analysis, Technology Play-Mapping, SPACE, the Company Radar Room and more. Who here is ultimately accountable? It's the Tenth Man or Woman who leads the professional SEAL, SWAT, RRT Rapid Response Team, or MI7 Intelligence Teams. The Tenth Man or Woman challenges

assumptions, leads with questions, and tells management the brutal truth!

We have a name for these outward-looking opportunity-mechanisms: strategic intelligence. The only place to position strategic intelligence in an organization is 'on par' with other functions that also report directly to the Board.

"The aim of strategic intelligence is simple: to deliver strategic intelligence that cannot be ignored to senior management"

"Strategic intelligence is critical for organizations to stay abreast of changing market conditions and to avoid costly mistakes. It is all about the proactive way of managing future-based risks in the dynamics of change in the external business environment"

IV   EPILOGUE

"Knowledge is a bunch of facts. Possessing much knowledge is not the same as being intelligent. Intelligent is not something you are; it is something you become"

"Learn how to see. Realize that everything connects to everything else", Leonardo Da Vinci

The above statements are relevant in today's business. Knowledge is not power, but shared knowledge is, which might make you more intelligent. However, we need connectivity to create intelligence. In today's world everything is connected. Smart companies make new connections because they realize that competing on their core competencies will not last. New connections are needed with companies which have the capabilities and attributes that truly distinguish them in their customers' eyes. Core competencies seem safe; but focusing on building core competencies is not the path to future business success. This is focusing on what those companies do well, rather than focusing on what customers want. What is needed is a new focus of outward-in rather than inward-out. I have described numerous examples of companies both those that behaved in this way, and those which did not. We are overflooded with data, information and knowledge, and management is not sufficiently able to create new insights and foresight from this: but strategic intelligence can.

A strategic intelligence team is perfectly able to support top management by building forward-looking strategies. Boards still spend too much time looking in the rearview mirror, while they should be looking further out than anyone else in the company. Too often we see in the media that CEOs are the last to see change coming. What is needed is to encourage a forward-looking mindset of the board of management. We propose of four ways to do this.

Firstly, the board must study both the current and future external competitive landscape. They must get the outside-in view of the industry as well as that from converging sectors of industry, from external sources, and also independently. Secondly, they must make strategy and strategic intelligence part of the board's DNA. At the start, the strategic intelligence team can help senior management broaden the number of strategic options. Discussions can then start on strategic alternatives and help select the preferred strategic direction. It is then, that the crucial decisions can be made. Thirdly, the board should use the full power of the top 40-60 talents in the company to organize quarterly strategy reviews. One of the toughest challenges in strategy development is the creation of different options. Questions are the lens by which problems are defined and addressed. Developing strategies is ultimately a people-centric process, fueled by conversation and dialogue. Each participant brings her or his experiences and biases to the table, and the job of crafting a strategy is to navigate those in a way that is productive. Fourthly, the board needs to anticipate the existential and potential future risks. Even the best systems and risk models cannot identify all the potential risks. This makes the role of the strategic intelligence team all the more critical.

Markets are reacting much faster than ever before. We see faster decision-making, faster information transfer, and tremendous interconnectivity. This is fundamentally changing the business environment, which makes it crucial to watch the dynamics of change in the business environment, 24/7, by establishing a Company Radar Room (CRR). Such a CRR should also replace the traditional boardroom, as it becomes the virtual battlefield in which the competitive war can be fought and won.

"We can only see what happened, not what did not happen. Although we can measure the behavior of the customers we have precisely, what about the silent voices of those customers we do not have?"